Cover: Panavia Tornado prototype P.06, XX948, at Farnborough, September 1976./*Denis J Calvert, Inter-Air Press*

Piper Cherokee Arrow of Ballyfree Aviation Ltd, taking part in an air race./*Peter March*

Second prototype MRCA Tornado with underwing tanks flying near its BAC Warton base at the start of tests to assess performance with a variety of external stores.
/British Aircraft Corpn

AIRCRAFT annual 1978

EDITED BY E.L. CORNWELL

LONDON

IAN ALLAN LTD

First published 1977

ISBN 0 7110 0815 9

Published by Ian Allan Ltd, Shepperton, Surrey, and printed in the United Kingdom by Ian Allan Printing Ltd.

One of Seaboard World's Boeing 747Fs disgorging at the London terminal./*British Airports Authority*

Contents

Small plane — big business 4

Tornado — the one-plane air force 25

Where now in Space 34

Japanese fighters of the Pacific War 46

Air Cargo's incredible variety 64

The avenging Grumman 78

Rust, restoration and resurrection 92

Dynairship — freighter of the future? 112

Collectors' Corner 120

Small plane - big business

ALAN WRIGHT

Early air taxi aircraft proved useful during WW2 ferrying Service pilots around the UK; the Fairchild Argus was one such and numbers survived to pass into civilian operation./*Alan Wright*

IN THE ERA of plus-fours and back-to-front caps flying of any sort was something of an adventure and, for most people, best left to those chaps with money. It certainly applied in the light aviation field, although the public followed the fortunes of the famous names with great interest.

The 1930s gradually saw the arrival of some fine British - built aircraft, particularly from the de Havilland, Miles and Percival stables. The last-named for instance produced the Vega Gull, which achieved fame while breaking many world records. It was later adopted by the Royal Air Force, becoming the Proctor, a machine which served until after the war in trainer and communications roles.

Although modern technology has allowed considerable advancements to be made in many respects with the production of small aircraft, some of those immediately pre-war types could match today's designs in all-round performance, not to mention lower noise levels. But like so many things, the outbreak of war stopped civil aviation development in the UK in order to concentrate on those aircraft with a more belligerent purpose.

This period did, however, demonstrate the usefulness of the small machines in a multitude of ways. The obvious need for basic trainers was catered for by thousands of Tiger Moths, Magisters and so on.

Above: Although fairly extensively used as a company aircraft the D4 Dragon Rapide served mainly with numerous airlines up to the 1960s./*Alan Wright*

Above right: The Stampe SV4 was released in numbers by French and Belgian armed forces and became popular in civilian hands, especially for aerobatics./*Alan Wright*

Right: A DH104 Dove 6 of Intrepid Marine International Ltd at Southend in 1974./*David Kingston*

Other important roles were played by Ansons and Oxfords, supported by many types supplied by America. The Fairchild Argus was a typical example, and one which was used with success by the Air Transport Auxiliary for ferrying aircrew around the UK.

The end of the war did not bring an immediate return to private flying. During hostilities a few civil-registered aircraft had continued in use and, airliners excepted, were mainly employed as company communication vehicles between their various installations. These types continued to be seen for the remainder of 1945, most of them shedding their sombre camouflage for brighter colours.

G-AXCZ
SV

IMI
G-BBYA

On 1 January 1946 the ban on private flying was lifted, an event awaited eagerly by the aviation industry generally. The first post-war civil instructional flight was carried out at Cambridge using a pre-war Tiger. The first private charter flight was recorded when Cambrian Air Services flew a cargo of wire rope and an aircraft seat from Cardiff to Bristol, for which task the company hired the prototype Auster Autocrat. Although only token gestures, at least a start had been made.

The next few years saw the UK civil register swell considerably with new allocations. RAF surplus aircraft began to appear in numbers, but so too did brand-new types. The Auster offerings, although based on earlier designs, flowed from the Rearsby factory, as did the Messengers, Geminis and Aerovans from the Miles plant at Woodley.

The private owner was not alone in acquiring a taste for the air. Business organisations began to make use of this form of transport, very often employing one of the Auster, Miles or Percival products. De Havilland produced the Dove, which turned out to be an attractive and sought-after aircraft for business and indeed airline needs. However, such was the state of the small carriers' finances that the mainstay of many fleets into the 1950s and even early 1960s was the trusty economic Dragon Rapide. It had continued its earlier success story while with the RAF during the war, after which it become available in large numbers and provided fledgling airlines with a cheap and reliable aircraft.

This was the pattern for many years, with regular boosts to sales as more redundant stock was released by the RAF. Although a boon to the purchasers, whether private or small business, it did little to encourage the UK aviation industry to provide new and inevitably more expensive hardware. Gradually the suppliers of British light aircraft withdrew from the scene, either without trace or to concentrate on more lucrative occupations.

This situation continued until 1959, when the import restrictions on foreign aircraft were lifted, much to the relief of those craving for a more modern machine than was currently available on the UK market. Immediately there was an increase of private and business aircraft on the register amounting to about 14 per cent. It is difficult to separate the two categories with accuracy, since some are registered to the businessman/pilot and others in the name of the company.

The majority of the types flooding into the UK originated in America, particularly the products of Piper and Cessna. The private and business aviation scene in the US had revived quickly after the war. The manufacturers had little difficulty in persuading the population to take air travel as an essential way of life as rail passenger services deteriorated and were withdrawn, while the great distances frequently involved in American travel have always made road journeys less attractive than in smaller countries, especially with fuel economy and safety speed limits in force. Moreover, the American weather is more predictable than that around the UK, allowing pilots to plan ahead with greater confidence.

In 1959 the sophisticated aircraft which started arriving not only looked sturdy new creations; they included radio and navigation aids, which in the UK was something new. Tiger Moths and the like rarely

Above left: The Piper Tri-Pacer became an early postwar UK import after the ban on buying foreign aircraft was lifted in 1949./*Alan Wright*

Above: A British-registered twin-engine Aero Commander at London Gatwick Airport in the early 1960s./*David Kingston*

possessed such devices — there was still an extensive network of railway lines to follow in those days! Needless to say, the acceptance of these modern gadgets did not come automatically. People are naturally averse to change, so it was a gradual swing in favour. As a result more and more pilots applied for and acquired instrument ratings, often at considerable cost to themselves. Nevertheless, even at that stage twin-engine British company transports were a very definite rarity, there being a natural built-in resistance to what appeared to be an extravagance.

Then someone introduced the word executive to replace business as applied to aircraft, from which point some advances were made. It is not really a true definition, since it implies that only the privileged few at the top of the managerial ladder can take advantage of private company transport. This is not so; most company aircraft are available for all authorised to travel on official business, subject to seats being free. The Philips electric concern, whose main base is Eindhoven in Holland, is a typical example of the larger-scale executive operation. The company has employed its own fleet of aircraft since 1955, steadily growing since that time. Its equipment has included a variety of single and twin piston-engine types, small jets such as the Mystere 20, a turboprop Fokker Friendship in the airliner category as well as helicopters. It has enabled well over 250,000 staff members to be carried on business trips, many to destinations outside Europe. With worldwide interests nowadays, the Philips Flight Division is capable of visiting any of the company's distant plants. Trips can be arranged at short notice if necessary, or itineries changed en route if the situation dictates, for maximum flexibility and utilisation.

The value of company-operated aircraft is now fully appreciated. The ability to avoid lengthy train journeys and the ever-increasing cost of overnight stays is of course common to the scheduled airlines. However, frequently factories and offices are well removed from the nearest airport from which convenient services radiate, so that the advantages of air travel are diminished. The smaller types of company machine can usually be stabled at a club field, or even on a privately owned strip within the grounds of the owner's head offices.

The prestige value alone is difficult to assess, but it cannot fail to impress customers when they are flown to their destination and later returned to their base quickly and with the minimum of fuss. A commercial contract is more likely to be settled satisfactorily face to face than by use of slower postal, or even telephone, communications. Costs obviously vary according to utilisation, size of aircraft, number of passengers likely

interstol
G-ASZJ
LOMBANK
Shorts QSTOL Skyliner
British Air Services

G-AVZG

Above left: Skyvan airliner designed by Short Brothers for short take-off and landing which first flew in January 1963. */Peter March*

Left: The Bell Jetranger turbine-powered five-seat helicopter introduced in the middle 1960s has sold well to companies and small airlines.*/Peter March*

Above: Bristol & Wessex Aeroplane Club Cessna 150, the world's most widely used basic pilot training aircraft. */Peter March*

to travel and so on. For most types of company aircraft operation it is usual for a professional pilot to be employed, replacing the owner-pilot of the smaller machines. Tax allowances and savings on fares are visible benefits, but time saving and convenience are worth a good deal these days. Once the decision has been taken that an aircraft would be a definite asset to a company, a considerable amount of thought and research must be devoted to the question of which types suit the requirement.

For the ordinary businessman pilot of limited experience wishing to take himself and the occasional passenger around the UK, one of the single-engine types available would be adequate. There is no point in acquiring complicated and expensive equipment if the piloting qualifications forbid their use except by a professional. The aircraft offered by Cessna, Piper, Beech and Grumman American are typical robust and reliable machines, as are the popular French designs from Robin and Aérospatiale. They are ideal for building up experience and of course are used extensively by flying schools and ordinary private owners. However, much will depend on the journeys likely to be undertaken and the estimated payload requirements.

If these comparatively slow types are not suitable, the next stage involves the provision of a more powerful engine and the refinement of a retractable undercarriage. There need not be a great increase in size but range, speed and payload will be improved. Nevertheless, a factor to be borne in mind is that the lower-powered machines can potter in and out of very small fields without fuss. The more lively types require much longer runs before daylight appears under the wheels.

While the small singles are quite capable of conveying small loads of freight, loading and unloading is not the easiest of operations on some. Passengers unaccustomed to flying or those who reluctantly take to the air are often not at ease with just one engine in front of their nose. Similarly the small fragile creation apparently strapped to their backs does not inspire confidence. Access to many aircraft in this category, and indeed some of the larger twins, is achieved by walking over the wing before the contortions to enter the cabin begin. Unsuspecting females can discover such manoeuvres to be a problem. A high-wing layout offers advantages in this respect.

It is becoming increasingly necessary for businessmen to visit foreign parts, entailing overwater flying from the UK. Certainly hordes of single-engine aircraft regularly cross the Channel without problem but for peace of mind the addition of an extra engine is comforting. If a case can be made for frequent journeys into Europe, then the purchase of a twin is worth serious consideration.

The increased benefits derived from such equipment have to be paid for, as there is a considerable increase in the capital outlay involved. As with the singles, the choice is varied, with the American manufacturers Beech, Piper and Cessna offering a number of models. Of these, only the Cessna 337 possesses a high wing, although some of the low-wing types, the Beech Baron for example, are equipped with a rear door for straightforward entry to the cabin. The 337 also differs in another obvious respect. The engines are fitted fore and aft of the passenger accommodation, with twin booms supporting the tail unit.

There are other competitors in this field, although none have the production capacity of the big three. The American Rockwell company offers its Commander range of singles and twins, all of which have proved popular designs. Unfortunately prices of all products from the other side of the Atlantic have increased regularly as a result of the diminishing British economy.

Italian currency, on the other hand, has also suffered devaluation, resulting in a reasonable exchange rate. The Partenavia P68B therefore becomes an even more attractive proposition. Although current models are fitted with a fixed tricycle undercarriage, a useful cruising speed at an average of 13 miles per gallon is achieved by clean design and twin 200hp engines. The appeal for the small operator is that it can readily be converted into a freighter.

Above the level so far discussed the twins become even more sophisticated and accordingly more expensive. The Piper Navajo for instance helps to bridge the gap between the light executive twins and commercial airliners. The Navajo is fitted with a passenger door at the rear of the cabin, complete with built-in steps. Cabin pressurisation of these executive types is now available, more usually in machines powered by turbines, but the need for such a refinement can only be justified really if the company aircraft has to make regular trips using airways to distant parts. As a consequence, fewer types in this category are to be seen in Europe than in America.

The ultimate in the choice of equipment is the jet-powered executive aircraft. As the humble pint of milk became the pinta, so did the lovers of abbreviations concoct the word biz-jet to define this class of machine. Not necessarily much larger than piston-engine types, the executive jet does of course provide a fast smooth ride over lengthy sectors in comfort. Interiors can be, and frequently are, laid out with boardroom furnishings, allowing business discussions without interruption during the journey.

Strangely enough, the jet's high-flying capabilities can prove a disadvantage, especially in Europe. As the regular air traveller knows only too well, delays can very often occur while awaiting take-off and landing clearances. Executive aircraft suffer in a similar manner when using overcrowded airways, with the result that speed advantages can be reduced significantly. Even on airline schedules the introduction of jets does not always bring marked improvements in overall flight times, but is merely often a result of public demand and the dislike of propellers generally.

With all the increase in business aircraft ownership, not every company has the need or indeed the money for such a possession, but occasions arise for all when speed of action becomes vital. The solution is simple — call a taxi. There are many air-taxi firms scattered around the UK who can normally oblige at very short notice, but there is still a reluctance by British businessmen to use their facilities. Maybe they do not know the local airfield exists or they forget the service is available. In other words chartering an aircraft is not an automatic reaction. Whatever the reason, the Americans and continental Europeans make far more use of air-taxi services.

One of the chief providers of employment for UK air-taxis is the conveyance of urgently needed spare parts or other stores. This is an especially valuable service for the motor industry where many factories rely on each other to maintain smooth production. Shortages of a particular item can be foreseen and flown in from another plant to avoid unnecessary shutdowns on the assembly lines. Other items which are regularly handled are flowers and fruit. Much of the early season crop from the Channel Islands and Scilly Isles reaches the mainland's markets in a fresh condition thanks to the small carriers.

Although always pleased to receive such work, the air-taxi firms naturally prefer contract charter operations, which apart from providing a steady predictable income enables fleet movements to be planned in a more efficient manner. The oil business growth in the North Sea opened up new opportunities for such charter work. When the bases were growing, much equipment and staff were flown in, which in turn triggered off the formation of many additional small concerns. Now that the oil companies are established there is not as much business available as had been expected. This coupled with improved services by the scheduled airlines, has forced the newcomers from the scene as quickly as they arrived. It has left the survivors to pick up the still not inconsiderable work.

Below: A French contender introduced in the early 1960s was the two-seat Jodel Mascaret of wood-and-fabric construction./*Peter March*

Bottom: Successor to the Tri-Pacer, the Piper Cherokee Six is used in thousands by clubs, schools, companies and private owners./*David Kingston*

G-A

Perusal of a map of the UK will rapidly confirm that the main trunk routes, be they road, rail or air, radiate from London. It is therefore a fairly easy matter to travel between most main towns and London but it is not so straightforward for those needing to venture across country. Improvements have been made, but regions such as East Anglia still remain difficult to reach quickly from the west. In these circumstances the air-taxi can eliminate tedious journeys in and out of the capital or other cities with little competition from scheduled carriers.

The benefits of the air-taxi have been particularly appreciated by the horse-racing fraternity for many years. Jockeys are frequently engaged to ride at two meetings in one day during the summer months and these can be as far apart as Newbury and Doncaster, but with many of the racecourses possessing air strips it is an easy matter to travel between the two tracks. The cost of the transport is very often shared between jockeys, who with successful rides consider the expense well worth while.

In order to maintain a high standard of operation, the air-taxi operators belong to an association set up to look after their interests. One of the agreements reached by the members was that only multi-engined aircraft would be used for passenger charters, flown by pilots with at least 500 hours in command. This experience is essential when operating into major airports or in foreign airspace. Normally it is accepted that no prior permission is necessary to undertake such flights, but several countries have insisted on advance warning, which defeats the whole object of air-taxi services.

In addition, customers sometimes use the facility to connect with their scheduled airline departure or arrival at the main airport. Some authorities encourage general aviation movements, offering good back-up services themselves. Others adopt the opposite attitude, which could force the taxi firms elsewhere, again reducing the effectiveness of the operation.

The aircraft employed by the air-taxi companies are usually from the American twin range previously mentioned. However, a few de Havilland Doves, and the bigger DH Herons are employed by some firms. It is rather surprising that the very successful Britten-Norman Islander does not figure more prominently in the taxi fleets. Perhaps its nine seats are just too many

Cessna continues to use a high wing in its smaller ranges, of which the Model 150 seen here takes a big share of the market./*Alan Wright*

Top left: Among the bigger executive aircraft is the turboprop Grumman Gulfstream 1; this one is operated by Ford Motor Company to link its European plants./*Alan Wright*

Above: The highly successful Hawker Siddeley HS125 executive jet; this one is a Series 3B operated by McAlpine Aviation. /*Alan Wright*

Top right: Sales of the Cessna 172/Skyhawk series have totalled tens of thousands since the original four-seat cabin monoplane was introduced in 1964./*Peter March*

for this type of work, when up to five is probably a more usual requirement.

The small twin-engine machines are not used purely by businessmen or air-taxi companies. Airlines operating scheduled services very often find that the traffic generated on particular routes will only support a small number of seats, making the use of a medium-size airliner uneconomic. Air Anglia for instance introduced a much-needed Norwich-Birmingham service on a twice-daily frequency using a Piper Navajo. The airline also used an Islander on a similar operation to Liverpool in earlier days, and the Fairey Britten-Norman product has really proved its worth on the more remote routes. Loganair, in Scotland, was one of the first operators, introducing it on its Orkney and Shetland services. The strips on these islands are primitive in the extreme, demanding considerable skill on the part of the pilot and reliability from the aircraft. Loganair operates the world's shortest scheduled service — two minutes between Westray and Papa Westray, a journey which often takes less depending on the weather. There is no cabin service!

A long way to the south a similar inter-island enterprise is carried out by Aurigny, which uses its aircraft to connect Jersey, Guernsey and Alderney as well as offering a link to Southampton and Cherbourg. Islanders were again the initial equipment, but they have largely been replaced by its three-engine development, the Trislander. A frequent service is possible on these comparatively short sectors, which are well patronised by residents and visitors alike.

The Scilly Isles have had a connecting air link with the mainland since pre-war days. In those times DH Dragons were used, giving way later to the Dragon Rapide. The Rapide continued in service in fact with various airlines, including British European Airways, until the early 1960s, when helicopters replaced the ageing biplanes. Fixed-wing services are still maintained to the Scillies, but by Islanders in the colours of Brymon.

One thing is certain, there is no point in having any type of aircraft without a pilot and the sources of those essential people are varied. Many are taught by flying schools around the country either just to private flying standards, or beyond into civil aviation as a career; others learn while with the Services and on return to civilian life put their knowledge and ability to commercial use. However, flying a Phantom or a Vulcan is one thing, a Navajo or an Islander another. Conversion courses are therefore necessary to obtain the required licences for transport flying.

Several establishments offer such tuition, ranging from full-time attendance for a year or two to correspondence courses. The largest of the schools in the UK are those at Perth, Oxford and Hamble. Airlines often send their new recruits to them for comprehensive training before becoming first officers in their employ. The college at Perth run by Airwork Service Training, provides accommodation for its large intake of students, who take up to two years to complete the course. Apart from flying training, engineering students tackle the syllabus for obtaining their appropriate licences for aircraft maintenance work.

Airborne training for the commercial pilot's licence

and instrument rating is carried out at Perth using the single-engine Cessna 150 and twin-engine Cessna 310. At Oxford the school is Piper-equipped, using mainly Cherokees and Senecas. Over 3500 students have qualified at Airwork since 1964 and it is now the largest such organisation in Europe.

After a period of service with an airline some pilots are attracted to company executive flying and smaller airlines are very often the source of supply for such staff. Certainly the wealth of experience required during an airline career is invaluable. Some ex-service pilots, and others undertaking the training courses without sponsors, choose business aircraft flying rather than joining one of the public transport companies.

The production of aircraft for the light aviation market has enjoyed mixed fortunes. In the UK the scene is practically barren apart from the Bulldog/Bullfinch series of Scottish Aviation. The Islander range from Britten-Norman continues to sell steadily and has become the most successful British design for a long time in its class. Executive jet purchasers have recognised Hawker Siddeley's HS125 to be an ideal aircraft to fulfil their needs at this level and it has earned millions of pounds in foreign sales alone.

However, although the rest of the world can compare favourably in efficiency and quality, it cannot compete with American mass-produced machines in terms of quantity. Cessna alone sold 7705 civil aircraft worth 405 million dollars in 1975. The very popular Model 150 series, carefully developed by the company over a long period from the Model 140 of the late 1940s, accounted for a large proportion. Construction costs have now been cut to a minimum and the US production line is capable of 10 aircraft a day. Most of the European Cessna singles are now produced by Reims Aviation in France, avoiding high dollar expenditure.

Above: The basic Piper Cherokee, the 140, which superseded the Colt in 1964. This is a 140C of CSE (Aircraft Services) Ltd./*Peter March*

Above right: The Fairey Britten-Norman Islander is used widely by third-level airlines as well as on air taxi and company work. /*Alan Wright*

Right: The Piper Aztec 250 twin has been found a useful machine for air taxi work./*Alan Wright*

Piper, on the other hand, changed from its earlier Tri-Pacer range of fabric-covered high-wing aircraft to the metal low-wing Cherokee, a completely new design that first flew in 1961 to compete with the Cessnas on more level terms. The Piper plant responsible for the Cherokee is capable of producing up to 15 each day, a formidable total indeed for just one type of light aircraft.

Compared with the thousands churned out by the Americans each year the remainder of the world's light aircraft industry does not build very many. However, unlike Britain, countries such as Sweden, Germany, Italy, Japan and France do have flourishing light aviation producers. The French Avions Robin plant at Dijon, for example, creates tourers in various configurations, some wooden and others metal. The company did not start operation until 1957, from which time it has expanded gradually. Although

HEATHROW
GATWICK
G-AXFC
WESTWARD

AIR
TAXI
SERVICE
G-AXFA

Above: Among the widely used twins is the Beech King Air; this B90 is operated by Winster Engineering Ltd./*Alan Wright*

Above right: Learjet LP1 on a demonstration flight over Hampshire in September 1974./*Peter March*

Right: Forney F1A Aircoupe of Cornwall Flying Club and, beyond, Beagle 121 Pup 1 owned by AAC Dingle & Partners at Bodmin in July 1975./*Peter March*

Next page: A privately owned Piper J3C Cub over Booker in March 1974./*Mike Jerram*

modern techniques are used, the factory still retains an unhurried atmosphere during the production of about 200 machines a year, many of which go for export.

A significant trend in recent years has been the increase in the number of company-operated helicopters. While the majority are flown by professionals, the small two-seat types are frequently flown on business by owner-pilots. The obvious advantage of the helicopter is its vertical take-off and landing capability. Careful consideration would have to be given before a company decided in favour of a helicopter in view of the high comparative cost. The deciding factor would no doubt be the type of business conducted, location of the main office and accessibility of outstations using surface transport, particularly from the nearest airstrip.

Movements of helicopters in the UK are controlled over cities and they must follow recognised routes. Operation of the machines from rooftops is only permissible with multi-engined types, the singles being restricted to ground-level landing sites. As usual the Americans lead in this type of activity, allowing a greater freedom of movement, with innumerable landing pads provided on the roofs of multi-storey car parks and skyscrapers.

All aircraft, whether winged or wingless, have to undergo regular maintenance checks, the frequency depending upon the class of machine, utilisation and so on. Many of the overhaul centres are operated by flying schools, clubs or air-taxi firms, and are officially licensed to perform the specialised inspections and repairs necessary. Sometimes, if there are several companies and private owners operating aircraft from the same airfield, it is possible for a pool of maintenance effort to be arranged, bringing together the required skills at reduced cost. Costs can vary widely but, like everything else, if an aircraft is neglected between checks a hefty bill is likely.

The employment possibilities for the modern light aircraft are endless. Crop spraying, aerial photography, road traffic observation and air ambulance work are but a few. The 20,000 or so holders of a private pilot's licence in the UK can either fly on fine Sundays for pleasure, or use their expertise in their everyday lives. The schools, maintenance organisations, licensing authorities, aircraft distributors, manufacturers of the hundred and one items of miscellaneous equipment required, airfield owners, air traffic control, etc etc are all part of the small plane scene. This scene will continue to expand because it has become an accepted, even essential, part of the modern way of life. It follows that it will also remain big business.

G-BBEE

G-AXNL
G-ARHC

XX946
XX946

RAUCHEN VERBOTEN
D-9591

Tornado - the one-plane air force

BILL GUNSTON

MOST PEOPLE may not know the story of the AFVG, the Anglo-French Variable-Geometry aircraft that in 1966 was the planned multi-role aircraft of the RAF. The British Defence Minister said it was 'operationally and industrially the core of our long-term aircraft programme.' When it was cancelled he said he had looked up 'core' in his dictionary, and found it meant 'the central part, normally to be cut out'. Those were dark days of political mismanagement, but somehow the planemakers of Britain survived and by sheer persistence and guts set course again and organised a new collaborative programme with West Germany and Italy. After looking at many proposals and projects the work settled on the MRCA (Multi-Role Combat Aircraft), which is now in production as the Panavia Tornado. And it is without much doubt the most important type of aircraft in the world, because upon it rests not only Europe's ability to defend itself but Europe's ability to produce advanced combat aircraft in the future. Upon no other single type of aircraft has been placed such a massive responsibility.

If MRCA had been a failure, or even technically second-rate, or very late in timing, or grossly over-budget, it would have been serious indeed for all the people of Europe. Though there are a few unthinking people who dislike its very existence, and keep shouting for it to be cancelled, most Europeans recognise that today it is foolish to be defenceless. Without Tornado the position of not only the RAF, Luftwaffe and Marineflieger (German Navy), and Aeronautica Militare (Italian Air Force), but of the whole defence of the West would be imperilled. Western Europe would rely totally upon American forces, and upon American design and manufacturing expertise, and in the matter of combat aircraft would become a mere builder of US designs, such as the F16. In fact the F16 and Tornado make an excellent pair, because while Tornado can handle most missions in all weathers, the F16 is designed primarily for air combat and is handicapped in most other missions by having a fixed-shape wing, one seat and shorter flight endurance. There are also many who consider two engines an advantage, especially for aircraft intended to penetrate hostile territory.

Tornado's design was based on the stated requirements of six NATO countries (the three industrial partners plus Canada, Belgium and the Netherlands), which at one time threatened to make achievement of a good single answer almost impossible. For example, if you want a good air-combat fighter it needs tremendous engine thrust, and a very large wing. This is just what you do not want for a long-range attack and reconnaissance machine, which needs small economic engines and a very small wing. During the crucial project-definition phase of MRCA, in 1969-70, senior staff officers and procurement experts from the six original nations argued their own cases until the result could have been a technical monster that could never have been created within a reasonable timescale and budget. Fortunately a few experienced men, led by 'Ollie' Heath at BAC's Military Aircraft Division at Warton, Lancashire, got out their pencils and plotted the requirements on paper. At once one or two requirements, insisted upon by single countries, stood out like sore thumbs. It was not too hard to get these cut down until they were less obtrusive. This made MRCA possible, and the result is not merely good but probably the greatest technical masterpiece in the history of combat aircraft.

It is very difficult to make a good multi-role aircraft, because, as I just showed, one mission needs qualities which ruin the aircraft's suitability for others. The answer is to make the aircraft very clever, with as many parts as possible of advanced design with variable characteristics. But this tends to make the aircraft complicated, expensive and so difficult to develop it is obsolete before it gets into production. To do such a clever aeroplane to a tight timescale and tight budget needs a team of engineers, test pilots and managers who can fairly be described as brilliant.

Today the menace of inflation is hitting the defence programmes of the West. For example, the B1 bomber needs a jettisonable crew-capsule, but will have ordinary ejection seats. It needs variable-geometry engine inlets, but will get fixed ones that prevent it

Above left: Panavia Tornado prototype 02 being made ready for flight at BAC's Warton, Preston, aerodrome. /*British Aircraft Corpn*

Left: Prototype 01 and its Turbo-Union RB199 reheated turbofan engine at the German partner's Manching, Munich, flight test centre./*Turbo-Union Ltd*

Above: Aircraft No 12, the second of six pre-series Tornados, after roll-out at Warton, with HF aerial glassfibre fairing removed for work on the aerial./*BAC*

Above right: Dramatic Tornado take-off on a demonstration flight at Farnborough 76./*BAC*

Right: Mr David Eagles, BAC Military Aircraft Division's MRCA project pilot, who flew the first British-assembled prototype, O2, on 18 November 1974./*BAC*

flying so fast, because they are cheaper. If Tornado was being started today it would be an inferior aircraft, because the development would cost twice as much. Fortunately it was started in the nick of time, before inflation really began to bite, and so it is a splendid machine that represents the very ultimate of what can be achieved with today's technology (or, rather, the technology of the late 1960s, because today's technology has yet to fly). From stem to stern it is almost totally uncompromised; it was designed to be as nearly as possible right for a wide range of combat missions. The result is an aircraft that several rivals can beat in one particular role, but none can even approach it in all-round effectiveness and efficiency.

Probably the most central key to such an aircraft is its engines. Perhaps the main fault of the original programme management is that the customers waited until the aircraft had been settled and was in detail design before even deciding upon the engines; in fact, of course, the engines should have been started about a year earlier. Turbo-Union, the company formed by Rolls-Royce, MTU and Fiat to produce the engine, have created in the RB199-34R-2 an engine of extraordinary versatility which alone is responsible for much of the outstanding performance of the Tornado in so many different missions.

The RB199 is an afterburning turbofan of extremely advanced design. There are three shafts, as in the RB211 civil engine, to give better handling and cut down the number of compressor stages needed to achieve the very high pressure-ratio necessary for fuel economy. The fan was based on that of the Pegasus, though it is much smaller, and several other Rolls engines fed in advanced but proven design features. The afterburner, however, was almost completely new, and it not only operates over a range of speeds and heights seldom required before but also gives augmentation up to well over 90 per cent — a remarkable figure — which in the sea-level takeoff condition raises thrust from 7500lb to 14500lb. Thrust is, of course, smoothly variable, without any sudden bangs or jumps in thrust as is still found in many engines in service.

In comparison with rival engines the RB199 is extremely small and light, and for almost every mission the total weight of engines plus fuel is lower than it would be for any other engines in the world, and lower than for any other aircraft that could fly the mission. The nozzles, of course, have to vary in area and profile to suit the different flight conditions. So do the air inlets and ducts, which have beautifully neat upper ramps downstream of horizontal double-wedges giving the best possible performance over the whole range of flight Mach numbers. Downstream the long and finely profiled ducts avoid engine/airframe

mismatch of the kind which so sorely afflicted the F111, though there are no inlet guide vanes and no variable stator blades of the kind found on almost all other advanced engines.

Most of the engine is of radically new construction; for example, the blades of the fan and intermediate compressor are welded in place. Without experience of both supersonic turbojets and ramjets it is doubtful whether Rolls-Royce could have developed the cunning afterburner with separate fuel supplies and flameholders for the core jet and bypass airflow. By no means least, the RB199 is — with the engine of the Swedish Viggen — one of the very few modern combat engines to have a thrust reverser. It is especially difficult to fit such a device to an engine with a high-augmentation afterburner, but the upper and lower 'target-type' buckets are hinged direct to the jetpipe and about the neatest ever seen. They are driven by pneumatic motors supplied with high-pressure engine bleed air.

These great little engines fit into an equally great airframe, which represents the very latest 'state of the art' at the time of its design. A multi-role aeroplane almost has to have a variable-sweep wing. The F15, F16 and F18 have fixed wings, and despite skilled design cannot reconcile the conflicting requirements of short-field takeoff and landing, combat manoeuvrability, long radius of action, Mach 2-plus performance and crew comfort in a low-level mission. In contrast, the wings of the Tornado are a joy both aerodynamically and structurally, and make one wonder why swing-wings seemed so elusive in the 1950s. Such a wing consists structurally of three parts: left and right swing-wings and the central wing carry-through box (WCTB). The Tornado WCTB which forms the structural heart of the mid- fuselage, is

fabricated entirely of titanium, welded by electron-beams, and serves as an integral fuel tank. It was designed by BAC and, although the first three units were subcontracted to Grumman because of delay in delivery of electron-beam welding machines to MBB, it is made in Germany by Panavia's partner in that country, MBB. (Thus, as MBB is Messerschmitt-Bölkow-Blohm and BAC incorporates Vickers-Supermarine, the Tornado is built by the people who built both the Spitfire and Bf109!)

At each end of the WCTB are the most vital structural points in any swing-wing aircraft, the main wing pivots. Each has four bearings one above the other, rather like meshing layers of plywood, the bearings, themselves being self-aligning spherical pivots lined with Teflon to avoid metal/metal fretting. The wings are positioned to any sweepback from 25 degrees to 68 degrees by a pair of long ball-screwjacks driven by a hydraulic motor, with an additional equaliser rod to ensure that sweep is always the same on both wings! In emergency the Tornado can land on any reasonable runway with the wings at 68 degrees.

The wings themselves are made by Aeritalia, the third Panavia partner, using conventional aluminium alloys in conventional ways. As is the case with most aircraft in this class the wings are really fuel tanks shaped like wings! In the early days of the MRCA the partners and their customers argued about whether there should be fuel in the wings, just as they argued about whether there need be two seats. In both cases I have no doubt whatever the right decision was taken, and all Tornados at present planned have two seats and 'wet' wings.

Flying controls are again really exciting. It would take too long to explain all details of the computer-controlled flight-control system, but the basic idea is that movements of the pilot's stick or rudder pedals generate triple sets of electrical signals. These are fed to the CSAS (Command and Stability Augmentation System), one set among dozens of 'black boxes' on board, which also receives signals from the surface power units and from rate gyros which measure response of the aircraft in pitch, roll and yaw. All the triple sets of electrical signals are compared. If there is any discrepancy the CSAS puts it right, and if one channel (one set of signals) goes wrong the other two outvote it, besides warning the pilot. The result is an aircraft that does precisely what it is told, and does it very quickly and smoothly. The electrical signalling is popularly called fly by wire, or FBW, and it offers many great advantages. The whole system also incorporates artificial-feel units, with automatic compensation for gross changes in aircraft configuration, external stores and atmospheric density,

Above: Prototype 02 carrying four 1000lb bombs and two large underwing fuel tanks as it neared the successful conclusion of the initial stores carriage programme./*BAC*

Above right: Prototype 06 carrying long-range fuel tanks on fuselage shoulder pylons during a test flight from Warton./*BAC*

Right: Mr Paul Millett, BAC Military Aircraft Division's chief test pilot, who flew prototype 01 from Manching in August 1974./*BAC*

as well as interfacing with the autopilot and computerised weapon-delivery system.

Even the surfaces themselves are not the traditional ones. The fin and rudder are conventional, besides being large to give good stability at supersonic speed and with large external stores, but everything else is done by the tailplane. In fact it is not called a tailplane, but is regarded as left and right 'tailerons', because they substitute for traditional ailerons as the primary control in roll, one tailplane being driven up and the other down. For pitch control, of course, left and right surfaces work in perfect unison. At low wing sweep angles, which means modest airspeeds, roll control is augmented by two sections of spoiler above each swing-wing.

The spoilers are very powerful, and on landing are flicked open right across the aircraft to act as lift-dumpers to allow the wheel brakes to be used at full power. With lift-dumpers open, maximum wheel brakes, two airbrakes above the rear fuselage like barn doors, and full reverse thrust the Tornado has amazing stopping power. Having no ailerons means the flaps can go right to the wing-tips, and they are extremely powerful double-slotted surfaces in four sections on each side. On the leading edge, right to the tip, are three-section hydraulically driven slats, while on the fixed 'wing glove' is a powerful Krüger flap which flicks open before take-off or landing to complete the high-lift system. It is probably fair to claim that no other combat aircraft in history has ever had such a remarkable array of flight controls and high-lift devices.

With the benefit of such outstandingly high lift in the 25 degree position the Tornado can take off carrying a load of bombs almost as heavy as anything carried by a Lancaster or Vulcan (one of the aircraft the RAF Tornados will replace). Not only can it carry a weight of weapons never before associated with aircraft of such small size but it will be cleared to carry a variety of external stores probably greater than any other aircraft in history.

Among the better-known weapons are regular bombs of nine sizes including the low-drag Mk 83 of nominally 1000lb, the German 'streuwaffen' (scatter weapon) and British BL755 cluster bomb, the Lepus flare bomb, various tactical nuclear weapons, a wide range of rocket launchers, the Sidewinder, Sparrow, Skystreak and Aspide air-to-air missiles, the radar-homing and TV-guided Martel, Kormoran, AS30 and

Above: Italian-assembled prototype 09 undergoing final tests at the Italian partner's flight test centre at Caselle, near Turin. /*Aeritalia*

Left: Mr Miller talking to Mr L W Dean, superintendent of the Warton flight sheds, with Signor P Trevisan, Aeritalia's MRCA project pilot, on the right./*BAC*

Above right: A model of the Tornado production line at Manching as it will be when the aircraft is in full production. /*BAC*

several other air-to-ground missiles (probably including Harpoon), and several types of fuel tank or flight-refuelling buddy pack (see 1976 Annual). Inside the lower fuselage are two IKWA-Mauser 27mm cannon of a new type specially designed for the Tornado. These guns have high muzzle velocity and can be set to a high rate of fire for ground attack or an even higher rate for air combat. Cases and links are blown through a duct and dumped overboard well behind the engine inlets.

External stores can be loaded on any of seven stations, three under the broad fuselage and four pivoted under the swing-wings to align themselves constantly fore-and-aft. Early in flight development in 1975 Panavia demonstrated completely uninhibited flight at 600 knots (691mph) with four Mk 83 bombs on two tandem body pylons and two monster 1500-litre tanks under the wings. Another (classified) load was demonstrated at full attack speed of 725 knots (835mph) at a height above the ground of 200 feet. This low-level attack speed is almost certainly considerably higher than that of any other aircraft in the world.

To make blind first-pass attacks at such speed — in other words to go straight to the right target and hit it without any need to search for it — demands not only a pretty skilled crew but also extremely comprehensive avionics. Full details of the Tornado's avionics may not be published, but apart from sensitive areas involving ECM (electronic countermeasures) and similar topics it has all been declassified. The main multi-mode radar is an American design by Texas Instruments, which in the terrain-following mode guides the speeding aircraft safely across the undulations of the ground at an extremely low altitude to keep as far as possible under the hostile radars. Primary navigation system is a Ferranti DINS (digital/inertial navigation system), and other equipment includes Decca doppler radar, Aeritalia radio altimeter, a laser target ranger or seeker, digital computer and very advanced HUD (head-up display) for the pilot and TV tabular display for the navigator, with a moving-map display for both.

I have still not covered more than a fraction of the interesting features of Tornado, such as the strong landing gears with the ability to use unpaved surfaces despite having single mainwheels, and the simple fuel system with just four internal tanks and a neat retractable FR probe. It goes without saying the Martin-Baker Mk 10A seats are the latest rocket assisted 'zero-zero' type, and they are singularly comfortable and easier to manage with only two safety pins instead of five. The canopy does not incorporate MDC (miniature detonating cord) but instead is blown off as a unit a fraction of a second ahead of the seats, with good separation ensured by small rockets on each side.

A liquid-oxygen system is provided for the crew, the pneumatic systems include provision for cooling the avionics even with the engines shut down, and also for pressurising the flexible seals around the roots of the swing-wings, while the two engines are mechanically linked by an accessory SPS (secondary power system) which couples the gas-turbine APU (auxiliary power unit) and accessories. Less obvious are even more sets of initials, such as the BITE (built-in test equipment) and OCAMS (on-board checkout and monitoring system) which virtually tell both the aircrew and the ground staff exactly where any fault is located and even help them put it right and check that the aircraft is fully airworthy again. The Tornado will be a dream to look after, but the only way this is externally evident is by the fact that so much of the outer skin is in the form of easily opened panels or hatches. It was a requirement that all main servicing areas must be reached immediately without the need for any hand tool.

Until 1976 the programme had moved rather more slowly than had been hoped, partly because of delays with the engines which would have been avoided if their development had been started much earlier. But in 1976 the programme really got into top gear, all nine prototypes flew (see programme summary in box), and flight hours jumped from 190 on 1 January to over 700 by the end of the year. Biggest milestone of all was the formal Memorandum of Understanding of 29 July 1976 when the three countries, having completed the latest and most searching review of progress made, agreed to go ahead with production.

Top left: First flight of prototype 02 at Warton on 30 October 1974./*BAC*

Above: Herr H F Rammensee (right), MBB's chief test pilot, congratulating German Government chief test pilot F Soos on his first flight in a Tornado in November 1975./*BAC*

Top right: Prototype 06 landing at Warton with the new Tornado assembly hall as a backdrop./BAC

At present the total number of aircraft planned for the three original countries is 809, made up of four preproduction machines modified to service standard plus 805 new Tornados.

The 809 aircraft will be allocated to the three nations as follows: Italy, 100; UK, 385; West Germany, 324. The Italian aircraft will replace the Aeronautica Militare's F104G and Aeritalia G91 aircraft of the 20°, 102°, 154° and 186° Gruppi in air superiority, ground attack and reconnaissance roles. The German aircraft will be divided between the Luftwaffe (211) and Marineflieger (113). The Luftwaffe Tornados will replace the F104G of Jabo 31, 32, 33 and 34 in battlefield interdiction, counter air and close air support roles. Those for the Marineflieger will equip MFG1 and 2 in strike missions against sea and coastal targets and for reconnaissance. The RAF will initially receive Tornados virtually indentical with others off the production line, apart from individual national avionic and detail fits, and will use them to replace the Vulcans and Buccaneers of Strike Command's 9, 12, 15, 16, 35, 44, 50, 101 and 617 Squadrons in the overland strike and reconnaissance roles. A small proportion of the aircraft for each country will be dual conversion trainers, with almost unchanged operational capability.

From the start, each part of every Tornado has been made at just one company, but the three nations each assemble and flight-test their own aircraft. The six preproduction aircraft which were coming off the assembly lines in the winter 1976-77 form the nucleus of an OCU (Operational Conversion Unit) for all Tornado customers at RAF Cottesmore. The basic problem of learning to fly the swing-wing Tornado has proved to be no problem at all — which is fortunate, because the United States refused permission for any Panavia pilots to be allowed to fly an F111 to familiarise themselves with swing-wings. By the time this annual appears the OCU will be in full swing, and to it will also have been delivered some of the first batch of 40 production aircraft. At first it had been thought these would include four for Italy, but in fact

it turned out to be 23 for the UK and 17 for Germany. Deliveries to Luftwaffe and Strike Command squadrons is to begin in 1978, with the Marineflieger and Aeronautica Militare following in 1979.

To complete the present story I must briefly report on the ADV (air-defence version), which is 80 per cent common with the IDS and will make up a high percentage of the RAF total; the original plan was for the UK to buy 220 IDSs (interdiction/strike) of the basic type and 165 ADVs, but no current figure is available. The ADV Tornado will serve vital roles in defending British airspace in place of the Phantom, and will have to fly long and arduous interception missions far out over the surrounding sea areas. It is not yet known whether it will have more powerful RB199 engines, or any other changes associated with operation in the air defence role from good prepared bases, but it has been announced that it will be equipped with modified avionics. Most important change will be a completely different radar, by Marconi-Elliott and Ferranti, optimised for the air-to-air mode and with extremely long range. One would expect to find an infra-red seeker as well, and the radar (or a secondary radar) would also have to provide guidance for the excellent HSD Skyflash missile, derived from the earlier Sparrow. Unlike the IDS Tornado the ADV will almost certainly carry four Skyflash missiles recessed under the fuselage, as in the Phantom. It will also carry Sidewinders or other short-range missiles, and the same Mauser guns. Externally the main change will probably be a longer and more pointed nose, though it is possible the fuselage itself will be lengthened to increase internal fuel capacity.

Altogether it is possible this version may eventually outsell the basic aircraft. On grounds of sheer cost/effectiveness the Tornado is certainly in a class by itself to any air force needing a true multi-role aircraft. In the 1980s its only Western rival is likely to be the F18, and this fixed-wing machine looks like being outclassed in all-round capability and price by the tri-national Tornado, the best one-plane air force in history.

THE TORNADO PROGRAMME

26 March 1969: Panavia Aircraft formed.

1 May 1969: project-definition phase.

October 1969: Turbo-Union formed.

Mid-1970: start of development. Avionics tested in two modified Buccaneers, radar in a Convair 240, complete engine installation under a Vulcan and gun in a Lightning.

September 1971: first run of RB199, at Bristol.

August 1972: completion of structural design.

March 1973: end of development, start of production (ie manufacturing) investment.

14 August 1974: prototype 01 (D-9591) flies at MBB, Manching, Germany; general handling and development.

30 October 1974: prototype 02 (XX946) flies at BAC, Warton, UK; flight envelope, handling and flutter with and without external stores.

5 August 1975: prototype 03 (XX947) flies at BAC; dual controls, high-incidence, stalls, spins and measurement of air loads in flight (a new technique).

2 September 1975: prototype 04 (D-9592) flies at MBB; avionics.

5 December 1975: prototype 05 (X-586) flies at Aeritalia, Turin, Italy; flutter, but damaged in January 1976.

20 December 1975: prototype 06 (XX948) flies at BAC; weapon and gunnery trials.

30 March 1976: prototype 07 (98-06) flies at MBB; autopilot and terrain-following.

15 July 1976: prototype 08 (XX949) flies at BAC; dual controls, radar and weapon-aiming.

December 1976: prototype 09 makes delayed first flight at Aeritalia.

First quarter 1977: first flights of preproduction aircraft (Nos 11-16, there being no No 10), two in UK, three in Germany and one in Italy.

Mid-1978: deliveries begin to service units.

Where now in Space

ARTHUR REED

THE COLD FASTNESSES of space could be said to have become a potential battleground on that day in October 1957 when the Soviet Union startled the world with the launch into orbit of its Sputnik 1.

Although the sputnik weighed only 184 pounds, its appearance in the sky, and its bleeping noise picked up by radio as it passed over, wakened the public in the West to the fact that future wars would not necessarily be fought in the traditional theatres of land, sea and lower atmosphere, and gave the military the access which they badly needed to the taxpayers' purse to counter the Russian threat.

Behind the scenes, military strategists in the United States had been aware for some years of the developing power in space of the Soviet Union. In an atmosphere of 'cold war', the Russians were known to be pressing ahead with the development of long-range ballistic missiles, and in 1954 the United States proved its own answer in tests which were conducted in the Pacific — an effective hydrogen bomb warhead small and light enough to be delivered by missiles to the heartland of the Soviet Union.

On 1 July that year, three years before the launch of Sputnik 1 awoke ordinary citizens to the new threat, the western development division of the United States Air Force Air Research and Development Command was set up in an abandoned schoolhouse in California with the brief to perfect in as short a time as feasible a complete long-range ballistics weapon system.

In the space of time of nearly a quarter of a century which has passed since then, both sides have established enormous space armouries which, due to the simple fact that they are there, have had the effect of keeping the peace. So far, space has not been used as a battlefield, but both sides are engaged in a constant race to ensure that the other does not steal a technological march on them which could lead to a

An impression of the United States Skylab space station with a service module docked./*via Jay Miller*

UNITED STATES

sudden pre-emptive strike through the ionosphere without the chance of retribution in kind.

In the same period the civil side of space has blossomed enormously, with Americans walking on the moon, assessments made of the nature of Mars, Jupiter, Venus and Mercury, with sophisticated satellites relaying back to earth a multitude of information on subjects ranging from the weather to mineral resources, and with men from both sides of the Iron Curtain working, and meeting, in space.

But whatever advances have been made in the civil sector, all have depended on military programmes for getting, quite literally, off the ground. The Eisenhower administration insisted, when it first established the American space exploration programme, that the civil and military sides would be conducted separately, and that the civil side would have a purely peaceful purpose. But it very soon became clear that civil astronautics had a vital need of the military side.

A Jupiter rocket developed by the US Army to boost missiles shot the first successful United States satellite into orbit, and from then on most operational satellites, both civil and military, have depended for launch on Thor, Atlas and Titan boosters developed for the USAF. All the astronauts in the National Aeronautics and Space Administration (NASA) manned space-flight programme were, from the start, military-trained test pilots. But US government policy continues to be to attempt to cloak much of the military effort in space behind the guise that it is for peaceful purposes; a prime example of this 'double-think' can be seen in the satellite programme.

The satellites now in orbit send back without doubt a wealth of information on such non-warlike subjects as pollution, plant diseases, forest fires, urban blight and, of course, the weather. But their main value to the United States, and to the West in general, is in military reconnaissance — a programme which has brushed aside the veil which in the past shrouded Soviet military activity, which has played a major part in

Three items of space exploration hardware from the Soviet Union, displayed at various exhibitions./*via Jay Miller*

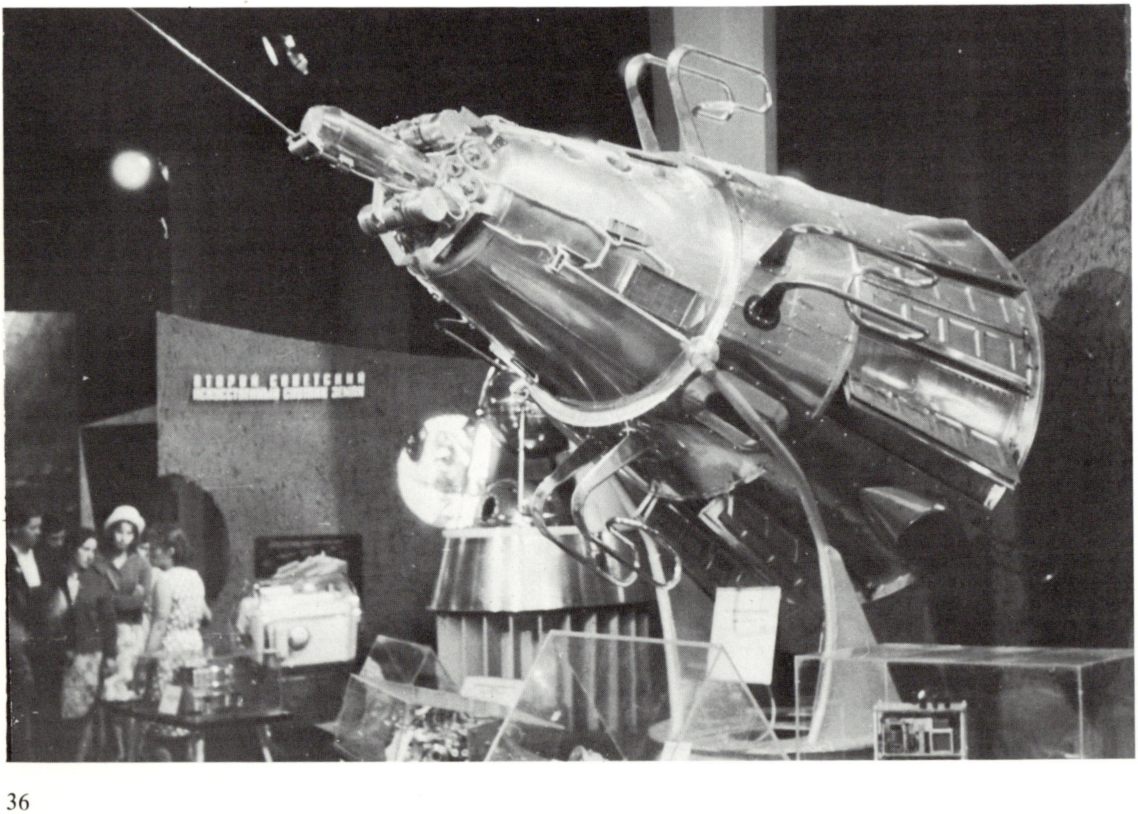

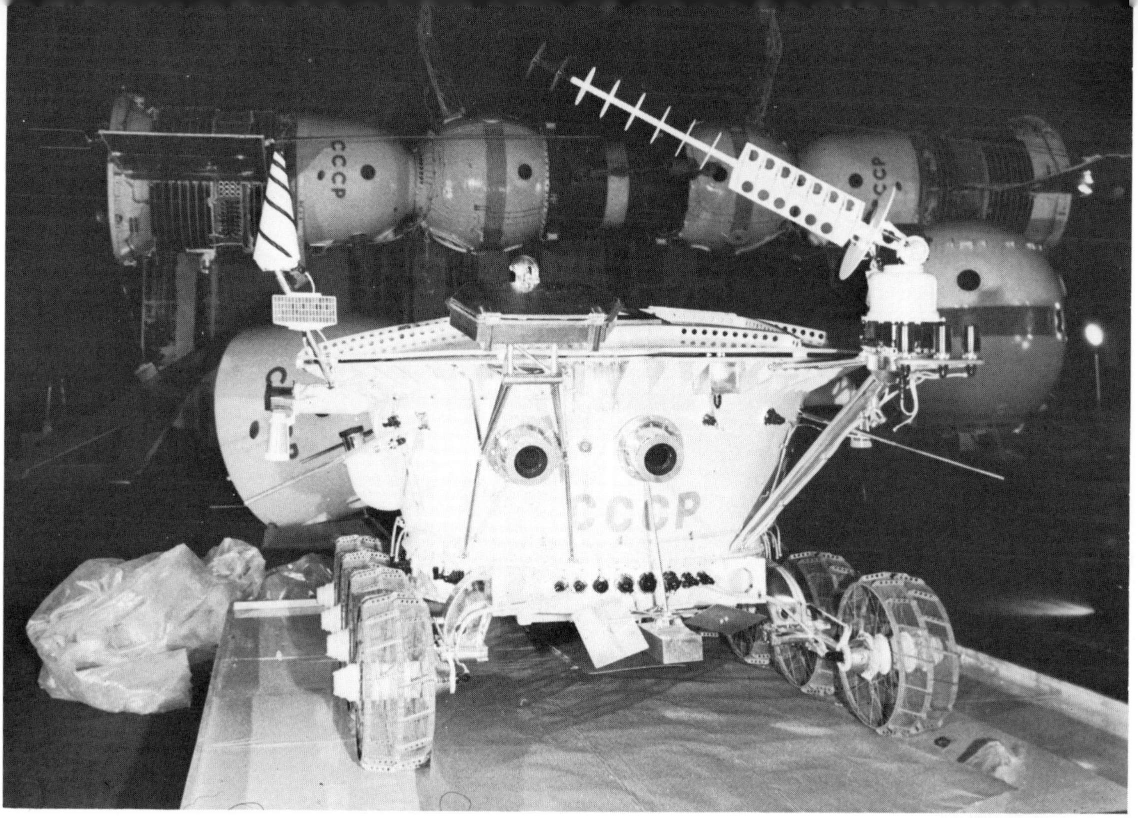
СССР

СССР
ВОСТОК

helping to keep the peace, and which has made U2 aircraft 'spy flights' as outmoded as Blériot.

Satellites — and both sides employ them — have been called the silent sentries, maintaining eternal vigilance with infra-red eyes from a beat 22,000 miles high. Through pictures which US satellites send down to earth observers deep in America can make out the numbers and even the make of a convoy of trucks in Siberia.

Troop, naval and aviation movements can be constantly monitored all over the world, but more important to the safety of the West is the ability of the satellites to warn of a missile attack early enough for a devastating reply to be mounted. All the while that this capability is retained by both sides the peace seems safe but, as is mentioned earlier, each side is constantly engaged in trying to erode the other's time in hand.

America now possesses military satellites able to detect, identify and track any missile or space booster within a few minutes of it being fired from almost anywhere on earth. The satellite system is backed up by the older but still very effective ballistic missile early warning system (BMEWS), the sea-launched ballistic missile detection and warning system (SLBMWS) and over-the-horizon radars (OTHR).

This warning network is backed up again by the NORAD space detection and tracking system, components of which include Spacetrack, a world-wide network of cameras and radars, and the Canadian Forces Air Defence Command's satellite tracking unit, which operates a telescopic camera used for photographing satellites.

Every day Spacetrack produces around 18,000 observations of the many satellites which are now in space. Since the launch of the first sputnik, no fewer than 7000 man-made objects have been propelled into space. Every one is logged; those which have been recovered, burned up upon re-entry into the earth's atmosphere, or which have collided with earth, other celestial bodies, or with other pieces of space hardware are catalogued as 'decayed'.

America's eye on space knows each one of those remaining, and knows also the path that each one of them is taking. What is known as a terminal impact prediction (TIP) is kept up to date so that the radars can be warned of space hardware returning to earth, and told what trajectories they are taking. The reason for such warning is obvious; without it, the returning space pieces could set off a false alarm in the missile attack warning network.

A further reason for tracking returning space hardware is that under an agreement which was signed in 1967 through the United Nations, each country is responsible for damage caused by its returning satellites.

The BMEWS chain owes its establishment to work carried out by scientists in the early 1950s at a time when tracking radars had a range limited to several hundreds of miles only.

Range was extended to 3,000 miles by using a high-power final radar output tube called a Klystron, and the first station in the BMEWS chain was built at Thule Air Base, Greenland, on the probable flight path of Soviet-launched intercontinental ballistic missiles. Working in arctic winds which reached 150mph on occasion, engineers completed the base in three years, erecting four antennas, each one larger than a football field. Thule became operational in October 1960 and was followed by two other similar sites, at Clear Air Force Station in Alaska, and Fylingdales Moor in Yorkshire.

Each site has a computer which calculates the

Left: A scaled rocket on test by ONERA, the French National Aerospace Research office./*Service Presse Gifas*

Right: Impression of the US *Orbiter* space shuttle being launched from earth with the help of its booster rockets. /*Rockwell International*

trajectory and parameters of any launch that it detects, and then assesses the probability that the launch constitutes a threat. For instance, a single launch might indicate a satellite firing or a test shot, and would have a low-threat value. Nearby simultaneous multiple launches would have a high-threat value and forces in the West would be alerted accordingly.

Even when a Soviet launch is discovered to be non-hostile, BMEWS interest in it does not end. If the new piece of space hardware proves to be an earth satellite, the chain will inform as routine the space defence centre in the US. The centre is a command and control system located deep within Cheyenne Mountain in Colorado, in a site hardened against nuclear attack. BMEWS, SLBMWS, satellites, OTHR and Spacetrack are all linked into this underground fortress complex which surveys and assesses, every minute of every day, all man-made objects in space.

The structure of the whole complex within the mountain rests on 2ft-diameter coil springs designed to minimise damage in the case of a nuclear blast. A tunnel leads from the outside of the mountain to two 25-ton blast doors which, in time of emergency, would be closed to seal the NORAD Cheyenne Mountain Complex, to give it its official title, into a completely self-contained unit. From there the commander-in-chief of the North American Air Defence Command would direct the defence of the whole North American continent. The complex can support itself without outside aid for more than a month.

Also located within the complex is the command post of the American global satellite tracking network, and also the missile warning centre. Information inputs from all over the world arrive at this and other defence centres by way of military communications satellite systems, which in turn play their part in keeping the peace by reducing the possibility of hostile surprise, and by shortening response time.

Under the control of the American commanders is what is known as the strategic Triad — a mixed force of manned bombers, land-based missiles and missile-carrying submarines. Backed up by the highly impressive early warning and assessment system outlined above, this becomes 'Triad plus one', formidable enough to deter the Soviet Union from launching a surprise attack — so long as the scales remain evenly, or reasonably evenly, balanced.

But the self-same system which has been established in the West to give warning of Soviet offensives also

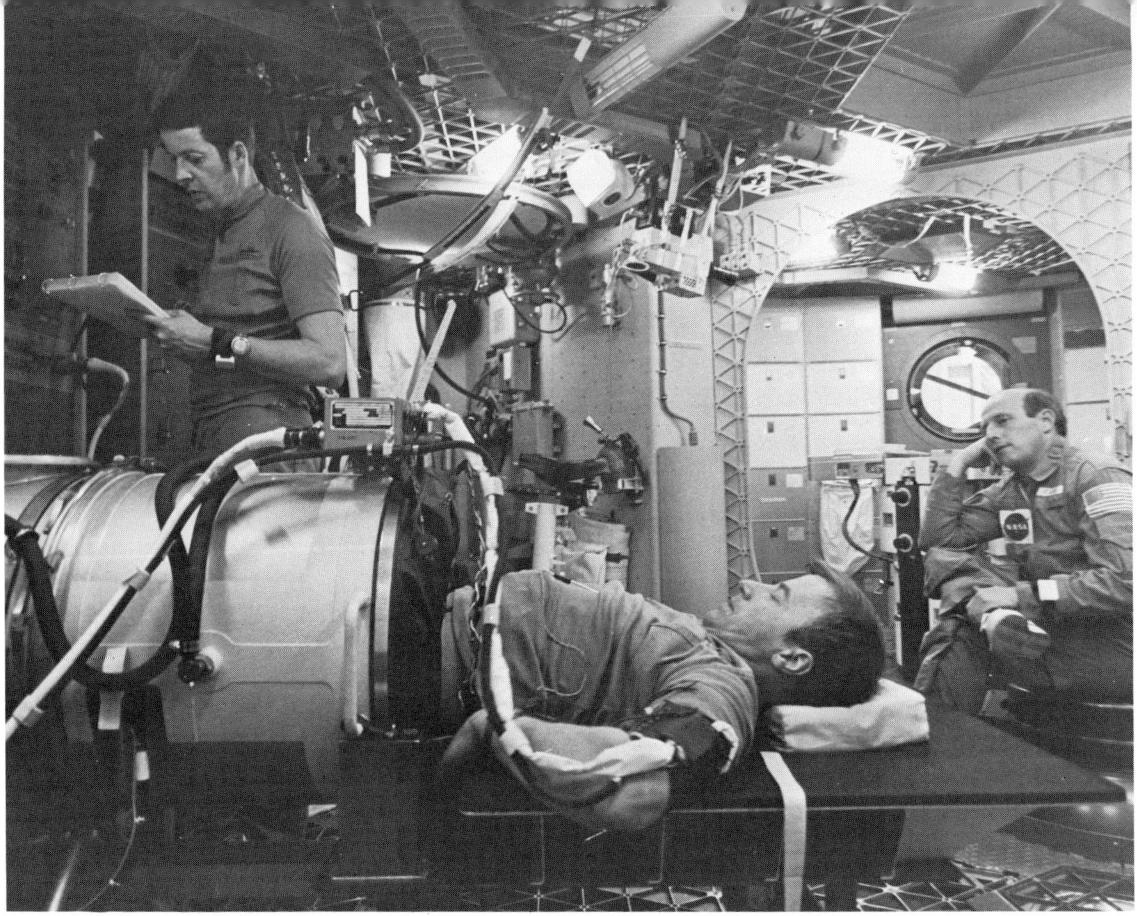

Above left: An American Skylab space pilot undergoing one of the many physical suitability tests at the US space centre at Houston./*NASA via Jay Miller*

Above: A representation of the American manned moon landing set up at the Smithsonian Institution, Washington. /*via Brian Walters*

Left: Another of the Skylab pilot's physical checks, inside a full-scale mock-up of one of the Skylab workshops. /*NASA via Jay Miller*

detects Soviet experiments designed to perfect a system of their own which will outsmart that of the Americans. Neither side has so far gone in for the tremendous national cost of a complete anti-ballistic missile system, but there now seems to be little reason why, in any future global conflict, each side should not be in a position to destroy the other's satellite eyes in the sky.

As long ago as 1970 the Soviet Union was observed conducting successful anti-satellite operations. North American Air Defence Command tracked the launch within one week of three satellites in the Cosmos series, numbers 373, 374 and 375. About four hours after the launch of 374 it was manoeuvred close to 373.

Cosmos 374 then suddenly disappeared from the tracking screens, and all that could be detected were several dozen fragments. An identical fate overtook Cosmos 375 when it was launched a few days later and was guided into orbit close to the first vehicle.

Early in 1976 the Soviet Union was seen to be conducting a further series of satellite interception tests, but this time the target vehicle was not destroyed. The intercepter vehicle was tracked passing close to it, and some western observers assumed that the purpose was to photograph it from close in rather than to 'shoot it down'. Others believed, however, that there was a malfunction in the intercepter's command avionics which made it impossible for its charge to be exploded as it passed near the target. It was noted that the intercepter satellite, Cosmos 804, was directed to make a sudden re-entry into the earth's atmosphere, and the theory was that the Russian scientists controlling it were worried that it would explode later at some uncontrolled time with damage to other Soviet or US spacecraft.

But although some experiments have failed, it is accepted by the West that Russia now has the capability of destroying satellites — a capability which the United States has had since 1963.

The latest American assessment is that the Soviet Union's system is extremely quick-reaction, able to be launched, rendezvous with and destroy a US satellite in less time than it would take the satellite to make one orbit. American satellite killer experiments were based on the blunter instrument of the nuclear-armed Nike-Zeus missile which, as far back as May 1963, was shooting down in test firings Lockheed Agena-D satellites in orbit.

An anti-satellite unit using nuclear-armed McDonnell Douglas Thor missiles was based under USAF control on Johnson Island in the Pacific up to 1975, when the unit was deactivated on the understanding that it could be brought back to full operational life in six months.

Soviet satellite-killer test firings have been few, but intelligence gleaned by US reconnaissance satellites indicates that they are ready to go into action at any time — and certainly not after a six-month warming-up period. Soviet SS9 boosters carrying killer satellite loads have been noted being wheeled from their hangars at the Russian space centre at Tyuratam, erected at a launch pad, fuelled and prepared for launch on a timetable that, on actual missions, would result in a firing from the pad in less than 90 minutes from the start of booster transport to the pad.

Above: Impression of the docking of a Skylab service module with the orbiting workshop./*RCA via Jay Miller*

Above right: The Orbiter shuttle will be coated entirely with 'tiles' of pure silica to avoid its destruction by intense heat as it passes through the earth's atmosphere./*Lockheed Corpn*

No details have been given, for obvious reasons, but the US is now working on the survivable satellite communications programme (SURVSATCOM) with the aim of providing worldwide command and control communications that could survive all phases of general war.

Work continues constantly towards refining the US satellite tracking and missile detection systems, the greatest spur to this work being the knowledge that the Soviet Union has tested a fractional orbital bombardment system (FOBS). This weapon can be launched to look like a satellite to the tracking stations, which would then give it a low-threat value. But after achieving a low-altitude orbit the payload could be abruptly deorbited and directed against targets on earth, so reducing drastically the warning time.

The FOBS system is a more sinister development of MIRV (multiple independently targeted re-entry vehicles), which both the US and the Soviet Union have developed, and which the US has in its space armour. They are booster rockets each carrying not one but possibly eight nuclear warheads which, on a signal from the ground, can be sprayed from space at a number of quite different targets.

What each side can put into their armouries is limited under the strategic arms limitation (SALT)

agreements. Currently the agreements permit the USSR superiority over the US in numbers of intercontinental missile launchers — 1618 to 1054 — and in submarine launched ballistic missiles — 950 to 710, while the US has an advantage in strategic bombers and in the numbers of warheads carried by its intercontinental ballistic missiles and submarine-launched ballistic missiles in MIRVs.

Talks towards a further agreement (SALT 2) are stalled at the time of writing, largely on non-space hardware, and in particular the question of whether the Soviet Backfire bomber should be classified as a strategic or tactical aircraft, and whether the US cruise missile should be limited in range to only 600km.

SALT 1 was signed in May 1972, in the recognition by both sides that they had the capability to destroy the other, but it was seen by both as an interim measure. In 1974 President Ford and the Soviet leader Mr Brezhnev agreed at the Vladivostok summit that their countries would work towards SALT 2, which agreement would remain in force until 1985 after the expiration of SALT 1 in 1977.

The SALT 2 treaty was to limit the total number of strategic launchers on both sides to 2400, and the number of MIRVed missile launchers to 1320 on both sides. The 2400 would include ICBMs, SLBMs and heavy strategic bombers, with each side being free to determine its own mix of weapons systems. Within a decade the number of launchers which each side has marshalled on the ground could become immaterial, as both the US and the Soviet Union will have manned orbiting space stations from which satellites, and also missiles, could be launched.

This significant new chapter in the space story is being written at the moment by the Americans with their space shuttle, the orbiter part of which was rolled out of its manufacturing plant at Palmdale, California, in September 1976. The shuttle was conceived largely

as a way of cutting down the escalating costs of the American space programme, for while every traditional booster which is used is lost in space, the shuttle can be returned to earth and used over and over again in a whole series of missions — at least 100, it is thought.

Shuttle was started as a peaceful project, but as indicated earlier, it is impossible to keep the military out of space developments.

The US Department of Defence will in fact invest between $1.5 billion and $2 billion in a share of the shuttle programme, the costs to include modification of the Vandenberg Air Force Base in California to accept the shuttle vehicle.

The Pentagon plans 10 shuttle missions initially, and the military payloads which are likely to be carried include (1) defence support programme early warning satellites; (2) USAF defence satellite communications systems; (3) US Navy fleet satellite communications systems; (4) weather satellites; (5) space test programme multi-purpose satellite, including laser communications; (6) laser weapons developed under a study which is now under way in the US to counter Soviet intercontinental ballistic missiles; and (7) long-wavelength infra-red surveillance sensors to detect low-flying aircraft like the Soviet Backfire bomber.

Above: Impression of the shuttle about to pick up an orbiting satellite for transport to earth or a space station for servicing. /*NASA via Jay Miller*

Above right: Illustration of how the Orbiter shuttle will carry the European Space Agency's Spacelab in its cargo hold and position it in orbit./*Rockwell International*

The shuttle orbiter is a craft 122 feet long, about the size of a DC9 airliner, with a massive cargo bay of 10,600 cubic feet which can carry satellites, or self-contained laboratories staffed with scientists and technicians who will ride into space in a 'shirt-sleeve environment' on the passenger deck. Standing on its tail for take-off, the shuttle will be blasted into orbit under the power of its own three main engines generating 470,000lb of thrust each, and two solid

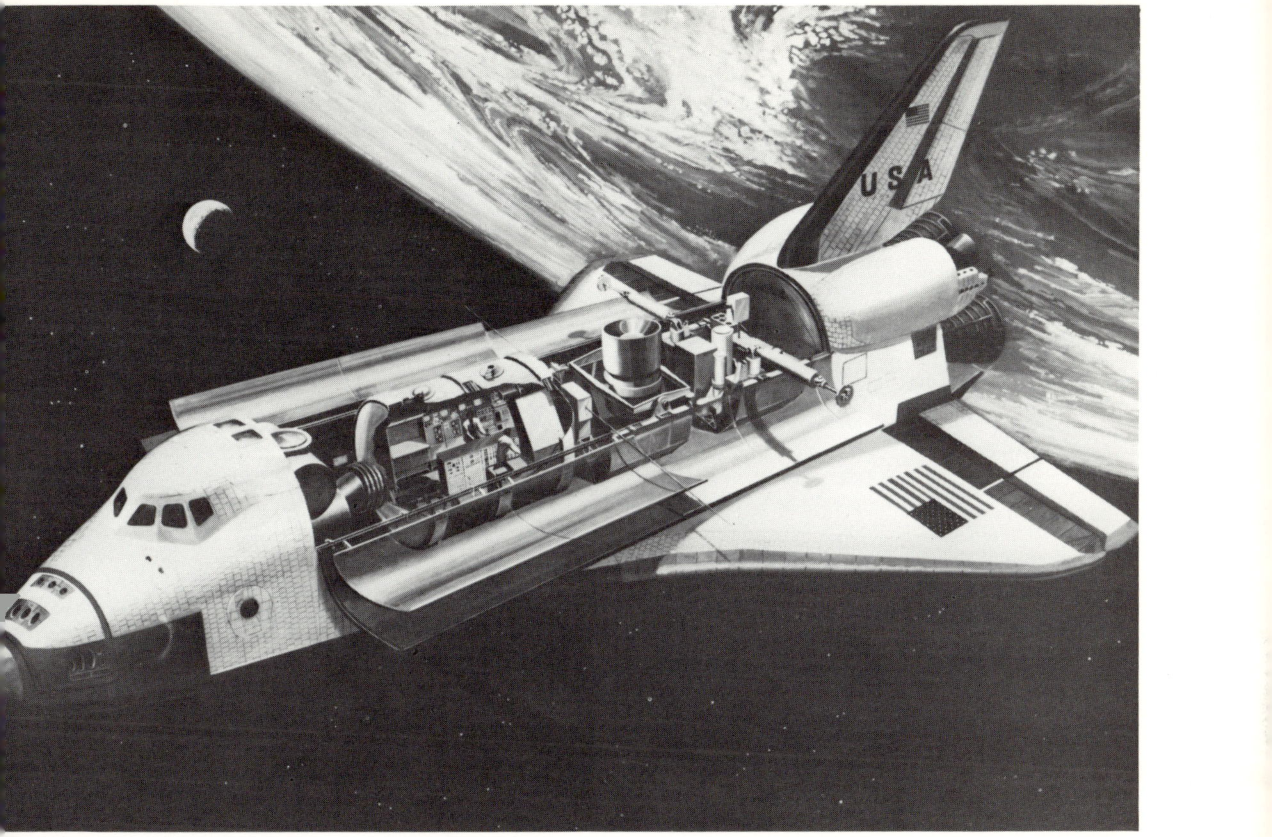

rocket boosters each developing 2,600,000lb of thrust. An enormous external fuel tank will contain the liquid hydrogen and oxygen ascent propellant to be used by the orbiter main engines.

The two solid rocket boosters will be jettisoned after burn-out at about 27 miles altitude and will be recovered by means of a parachute system. The large external fuel tank will be cast off before the shuttle goes into orbit. The orbital manoeuvring system of the orbiter vehicle will be used to attain the desired trajectory in space and to make any further changes of course required throughout the mission.

Once installed in orbit, the crew will begin their payload operations which, in addition to the military tasks mentioned above, will range from launching satellites to assist in earth resources surveys and improved navigation at sea to scientific and medical experiments and even manufacturing in space.

With the orbital operations complete the shuttle will re-enter the earth's atmosphere at a high angle of attack. At low altitude it will move into horizontal flight for a normal airliner-type approach and wheels-down landing on an airport runway. After touchdown the orbiter will be towed to a maintenance hangar where it will be cleaned and refurbished in preparation for its next sortie into space two weeks later.

A Boeing 747 is being prepared at present to lift the first orbiter vehicle on its back so that the orbiter can carry out airfield approach and landing trials. A second orbiter should be ready for launching into earth orbit for six test missions in 1979 and 1980.

Rockwell International, the US company developing the shuttle, is confident that on blast-off the occupants, a crew of four and six passengers, will be subjected to a gravity load of no more than 3G, and on re-entry to no more than 1.5G. This will mean that men and women without astronaut training will be able to accompany shuttle missions. As NASA has already indicated that there could be as many as 570 space shuttle missions in the next decade, it is clear that space in the middle and distant future will become as everyday an environment for human beings as is the lower atmosphere today.

It also seems inevitable that with such ease of access, the military will make more and more use of this new territory so that events on earth will tend to be more and more shaped by who has control over the void thousands of miles above.

Japanese fighters of the Pacific War

MALCOLM PASSINGHAM

All pictures in this article supplied by author

WHEN IMPERIAL JAPAN launched her all-out attack on 7 December 1941, with the intention of bringing the Pacific and the whole of South-East Asia under her control in less than a year, her Army and Navy fighter arms depended almost exclusively on two very typical single-seat aircraft. The Army fighter sentais (equivalent to RAF wings) and independent chutais (squadrons) with the exception of just three units were equipped with the Nakajima Type 97 fighter, which had won its spurs fighting the Russians at Nomonhan in 1939. A very small low-wing monoplane with enclosed cockpit, single-strut spatted undercarriage and radial engine, the Type 97 (or Ki27) was still little known to its British and American victims. The Navy had an even greater surprise for its new enemies, the Mitsubishi Type O carrier fighter, soon to become famous as the Zero to the Allies, and the Reisen to the Japanese.

The Zero had flown for the first time on 1 April 1939, piloted by Katsuzo Shima. It had been built to a 12-Shi (12th year of the Showa dynasty = 1937) specification issued by the Navy on 19 May 1937. In the light of combat experience the specification was revised in October the same year. It required the new carrier fighter to be capable of achieving 311mph (500km/h) at 13,125ft (4000m), to have an endurance of at least six hours at cruising speed and utilising a drop tank, to take off in 230ft (70m) with a 27-knot headwind and to carry heavy machine gun and cannon armament. The rival Nakajima company, somewhat daunted and overburdened with other design work, at that stage withdrew from the contest.

During testing of the first prototype, designated A6M1, the two-blade variable-pitch propeller was replaced by a three-blade constant-speed unit and all the Navy requirements were met except for the top speed. The third prototype and subsequent aircraft

Kawasaki Hien of the 37th Sentai.

05

Above: A line of Mitsubishi Navy Type O Model 21 carrier fighters being serviced, showing manually folded wingtips.

Left: A formation of Mitsubishi Navy Type 96 fighters of the 12th Kokutai over Hankow in 1938.

Right: A Type O Model 52 with insignia covered, being flown for aircraft recognition photographs after capture by US forces.

had the Nakajima Sakae radial engine in place of the less powerful Mitsubishi Suisei of 875hp. Designer Jiro Horikoshi and his team then saw all their expectations exceeded. A batch of service trials aircraft was built as the A6M2 (A = carrier-borne single-seat fighter, 6 = sixth design in that category accepted by the Japanese Navy; M = Mitsubishi; 2 = second major variant) and 15 fighters went to the 12th Rengo Kokutai (Combined Air Corps) in China. From September 1940 for a year, until redeployed for the attack on the Allies, they wrought havoc in China, claiming 99

Chinese aircraft destroyed for the loss of only two Zeros to ground fire. The A6M2 proved to be fast and manoeuvrable and to have good serviceability

In the West poor intelligence and lack of communication kept the Air Force commanders in ignorance of the new fighter, yet it was a key weapon with the units which launched the two-pronged attack on Pearl Harbour and the Philippines on 7 December 1941. The Zeros flying from the carriers of the Combined Fleet escorted Type 97 attack bombers and Type 99 dive bombers to Pearl Harbour and they succeeded in two brief hours over Hawaii in destroying the considerable US Army and Navy air units based there, thus ensuring the safe withdrawal of the Japanese naval units without fear of counter-attack from the air. The Combined Fleet Zeros then went on to victory over Wake and Darwin and on into the Indian Ocean to Ceylon, where the carrier HMS *Hermes* was sunk and many RAF and Fleet Air Arm aircraft were destroyed. Many other Zeros were attached to the land-based 11th Koku Kantai (air fleet) and engaged the British, Americans and Dutch during the conquests of the Philippines and the Netherlands East Indies.

Even so, there were only 328 A6M2s on strength on that first day of war. They were supported by a number of the elderly Mitsubishi Type 96 carrier fighters — the A5M4, a low-wing aircraft powered by a Nakajima Kotobuki radial engine of only 550hp. The Type 96 prototype had flown in early 1935 and the type had given a good account of itself over China. A low-wing open-cockpit (except for the A5M2a version) fighter with a spatted single-strut undercarriage, it was almost as manoeuvrable as its biplane predecessors while offering an excellent maximum speed for the period of 270mph (435kmh). By late 1941, however, the Type 96 (Allied code name Claude) equipped only the koku sentais (carrier divisions) aboard the carriers *Ryujo, Zuiho* and *Hosho*. They were to cover Formosa-based Type 96 and Type 1 twin-engine bombers overflying the Pacific from their bases in Formosa to attack the Philippines, but in the event the excellent range of the Reisens with drop tanks flying from Formosa as escort to the bombers attacking their targets on Luzon, about 500 miles away, rendered support by the Type 96s unnecessary. The only recorded use of the Type 96 against the Allies was in the assault on Davao, the principal city of Mindanao in the south of the Philippines.

Just 20 months after the first flight of the Navy's Type 96, the Nakajima Ki27 Army fighter prototype took the air, on 15 October 1936. It went on to eliminate the Kawasaki Ki28 and the Mitsubishi Ki33 (a variant of the A5M) from the design contest on the strength of its superior manoeuvrability. Production followed the pre-series batch of 10 Type 97 fighters, as they were by then designated, during 1937 and a grand total of 3398 was produced. The Type 97 reached a top speed of 292mph at 11,480ft (470km/h at 3500m) and could climb to 16,405ft (5000m) in just over five minutes. Fitted with blister drop tanks

between the undercarriage legs, the Type 97's range was boosted to 1060 miles. The performance was achieved by utilising a very light structure, weighing just 3946lb (1790kg) in normal loaded condition. While the Type 97 was best known for its service in Malaya and later in Burma, it was active wherever Japanese Army units were engaged and was not supplanted by the Nakajima Type 1 as the principal Japanese Army fighter until late 1942. At its peak the Type 97, by then coded as Nate by the Allies, equipped 22 sentais (each with between 30 and 50 aircraft) and five independent chutais (with between nine and 12 aircraft each). The sentai normally comprised three chutais and headquarters section (sentai hombu). During the occupation of Malaya and the invasion of Burma, the Type 97 equipped the 1st, 11th, 21st, 64th and 77th Sentais and top-scoring Army pilots Saburo Togo (commander of the 1st Sentai) and Tateo Kato (of the 64th Chutai) won many of their victories on the type.

It is now proposed to look at the Mitsubishi Type O carrier fighter, the Zero, whose early years of service gave it an air of invincibility, in greater detail. The design of the Zero showed an approach uncluttered by preconceived notions, but taking into account solely the anticipated needs of Japanese Navy fighter pilots. The war was not to last long; Navy leaders confidently forecast that it must be won in a year, and if it was not then disaster was inevitable. And so it proved!

Therefore, an aggressive posture was essential. Zero fighters would be concentrated in areas destined for immediate attack, thus achieving numerical superiority, or at least equality, and they must be capable of obtaining and maintaining control of the air over an enemy forced permanently on the defensive.

Above: Type O Model 53Cs of the Genzan Kokutai early in 1945.

Above right: A Mitsubishi Navy intercepter J2M3 Thunderbolt.

Right: A Kawanishi Navy intercepter N1K2-J Violet Lightning, showing factory marking on tailplane.

The navy fighter must take off and land in relatively short distances and be capable of good control during landing on carrier decks. It must be highly manoeuvrable — the first and great priority of Japanese fighter pilots, whether Navy or Army; it must have a good turn of speed and reasonable rate of climb; it must be heavily armed with cannons as well as machine guns; and the pilot must have excellent visibility in the air, on the ground and on the flight deck. Whether it was the Samurai spirit or the concept of a short always-attacking war, no attention was paid initially to protection of the pilot or fuel tank. The Zero was the first mass-produced fighter to have an all-round-vision cockpit canopy; it was built from a new ultra-light alloy — Sumitomo ESD, which was soon to be copied by other countries. The fuselage comprised two monocoque structures. The forward section ended immediately behind the pilot's cockpit where it was bolted to the rear section which tapered neatly to the tail. The wings and tailplane were

carefully faired into the fuselage and attachment was by simple bolting methods. The engine cowling was efficiently contoured to the fuselage. The result was a remarkably pure profile. The wing had Mitsubishi 118 section and was built up on two main spars. The undercarriage retracted inwards to lie wholly within the wing profile, while both the tailwheel and arrester hook were retractable.

As the land-based kokutais (naval air corps) dominated the skies in the rapid conquests of the Philippines and the Dutch East Indies, Japanese Navy pilots built up a tremendous toll of Allied aircraft shot out of the skies. Foremost among them was Petty Officer Saburo Sakai of the Tainan Kokutai who in eight months of operational flying destroyed no fewer than 60 American, Dutch and Australian aircraft before severe wounds suffered in an attack on Grumman TBF1 Avengers forced his retirment from front-line combat. Carrier-based Reisens were no less successful, giving support to the task forces moving through the South Pacific and Indian Oceans.

Prior to December 1941 a number of modifications were incorporated on the Zero assembly lines at Nagoya, from the 22nd A6M2 the rear spar was reinforced and from the 65th machine folding wingtips were introduced because the fully extended wings, spanning 39ft 4½in (12m), were too wide for the lifts on Japanese carriers. In April 1941 the problem of aileron flutter was resolved by fitting a tab and from then onwards production proceeded smoothly at the Mitsubishi factory, which went on to build 804 A6M2s until the Model 22 was finally supplanted on the assembly lines in mid-1944. Nakajima had also joined the production programme during 1941.

By as early as mid-May 1942, however, events were turning the tide against Japan. The Battle of the Coral Sea that month resulted in almost equally heavy losses on both sides, but to the Japanese Navy's Air Force the considerable toll of skilled pilots and front-line aircraft could not be made good immediately and the planned invasion of Australia had to be abandoned. Then, with the Zero playing a defensive role, came Midway, a massacre in which all four Japanese carriers engaged, the *Kaga, Akagi, Soryu* and *Hiryu,* were sunk for the loss of a single US carrier. American air losses were heavy, but many were obsolete aircraft, while the Japanese lost all their valuable carrier aircraft and most of their irreplaceable veteran aircrews.

From then onwards the tables were truly turned. The Zero had been an excellent aggressive weapon in the hands of experienced and dedicated pilots engaging a demoralised enemy. For six months and more Allied pilots had to be content with a motley collection of Curtiss-Wright 21Bs, Brewster Buffalos, Curtiss P36A Mohawks and Bell P39D Airacobras, most of them falling far below the exaggerated sales-publicity claims of their manufacturers. The rugged Grumman F4F Wildcat and Curtiss P40 alone had held their own and it was with later versions of these types that the fight back began. It was not too long before they were to be joined by other American fighters of higher performance, which gave priority to speed and to pilot and fuel protection.

There had been efforts to develop a carrier-borne Japanese fighter to supersede the Zero as early as 1940, but 16-Shi and 17-Shi specifications issued in 1941 and 1942 finally resulted in the Mitsubishi A7M Reppu (Hurricane). Development problems, an earthquake and finally the toll exacted by Superfortress raids, delayed progress. By the war's end just 10 examples of Reppu (identified by Allied Intelligence and coded Sam) had been finished, most of them prototypes. Nevertheless, the planned carrier fighter Reppu Model 22, had the war lasted a few months longer, would have appeared in numbers enough to worry the Allies, with an estimated 390mph at 21,655ft (628km/h at 6600m), climb to 19,685ft (6000m) in six minutes seven seconds and an armament of four wing 20mm cannons.

In the enforced absence of a Zero replacement, however, the original design was improved by all possible means. The Type O Model 32 (A6M3) entered service towards the end of 1942 and fought over the Solomons and New Guinea. The Sakae Model 21 engine gave 1130hp for take-off and slightly higher speed and generally enhanced performance at medium altitude were attained. The most obvious external change was a shorter wing with square clipped tips. The Model 32 proved less stable in carrier take-offs and landings than its predecessor and it was accordingly directed to the land-based Navy kokutais.

The major production model of the second part of the war was the Model 52 (A6M5). There was no alternative powerplant, but individual exhaust stacks gave augmented thrust. The Model 32 wingspan was retained, but the wingtips were rounded as in the Model 22. At last armoured glass was provided for the pilot and automatic fuel tank fire extinguishers were fitted. Performance, except for range, was better, but it was all to little avail and the Hellcats of the US Navy destroyed large numbers of A6M5bs during the 'Marianas Turkeyshoot'. By the time the Philippines was reoccupied most of the large Zero force there had been eliminated. Later versions of the Zero — the A6M7 fighter-bomber variant and the A6M8 with the powerful Mitsubishi Kinsei 62 engine — remained as prototypes. The Zero saw out its career equipping the bulk of the home-defence Navy units, and was hastily modified for night-fighting and Kamikaze attacks. From mid-1943 onwards it was definitely outclassed and did little to stem the inexorable Allied advance.

Looking at the Zero progression through its career the wingspan of production Model 32 and 52 fighters was just one metre less than that of the Model 22. Loaded weight crept steadily up from 5313lb for A6M2 to 5609lb for A6M3 and 6025lb for A6M5. Top speed rose from 331mph to 338mph and then to 351mph for the Model 52.

Back in 1938 the Japanese Naval Air Command had realised the value of a specialised target-defence intercepter with good top speed and climb characteristics, while providing pilot protection. The Zero's designer, Jiro Horikoshi, developed the J2M prototype to a 14-Shi specification and the smooth-profiled tubby low-wing fighter, with its distinctive shallow curved windscreen canopy and powered by a Mitsubishi Kasei radial, first flew on 20 March 1942. Bold efforts to achieve high performance — a laminar-flow aerofoil section and a tapered engine cowling, requiring an extension shaft to drive the propeller, resulted in a prolonged development period. Finally, with a Kasei 23a engine (replacing the Kasei 13) and a shortened engine cowl, test pilot Katsuzo Shima expressed himself satisfied with the new fighter.

Then disaster followed; two prototypes crashed out of 14 J2Ms produced by April 1943. After the causes were ascertained — and corrected — the tailwheel fouling the elevator control rods during retraction, preventing the pilot from pulling out of a dive — production got under way, still very slowly. First aircraft went to the 381st Kokutai in Japan, but only about 500 of all versions were ever completed. The J2M was dubbed Raiden (Thunderbolt) by the

Japanese Navy and was coded as Jack by the Americans. The chief variant, the J2M3, equipped the 302nd, 332nd, 352nd as well as the Genzan and Tainan Kokutais. Encountered over the Philippines as well as over the homeland, the Raiden was always treated with respect by Allied pilots. It reached 365mph (587km/h) at 17,390ft (5300m) and climbed to 19,685ft (6000m) in six minutes 14 seconds.

The Kawanishi intercepter fighter Shiden (Violet Lightning) Model 11 had an unusual ancestry. In planning an aggressive war, the Japanese Navy commanders had assumed that inevitably in a campaign involving thousands of islands they would at certain stages be deprived of the use of landing strips while at the same time being unable to call upon carriers for fighter support. They concluded that a floatplane fighter was the only answer. The portly Kyofu (Mighty Wind) floatplane fighter was accordingly developed, designated N1K1. Its evolution was protracted and as a stop-gap the A6M2-N adaptation of the Zero was introduced. A total of 327 was built and the type, which attained 270mph (434km/h) at 16,405ft (5000m), was used operationally in the Aleutian and Solomon Islands, at opposite ends of the Pacific Ocean.

The A6M2-N and Kyofu both had a large central float with a pair of wingtip floats. Kyofu production ceased in March 1944 after only eight prototypes and 89 production machines had been completed. It was

Right: Nakajima Army Type 97 Model B fighter in wartime paint just after outbreak of the Pacific War.

Below: Nakajima Army Type 1 Model 2KAI on skis in Manchuria in 1944.

assigned to Balikpapan in Borneo and finally in 1944 to a homeland air defence unit operating from Lake Biwa. The Kyofu attained a remarkable 304mph (489km/h) at 18,700ft (5700m), but still was not an operational success. Kawanishi engineers were, however, quick to realise the potential of a landplane fighter based on the floatplane.

Four N1K1-J landplane prototypes, powered by 1920hp radials, had been built by July 1943. The tubby streamlined fuselage and mid-wing arrangement were retained, thus necessitating a long stalky undercarriage which soon gave trouble, both due to its tendency to collapse and to the awkward 'sit' it gave the aircraft on the ground which impeded the pilot's view when taxying. The good top speed of 357mph (575km/h) and outstanding flight characteristics nevertheless interested the Navy and the production of additional prototypes and service trials aircraft was accordingly authorised, 70 appearing by the end of 1943. Quantity production followed and the type achieved prominence over Cebu in thc Philippines with thc 201st Kokutai. Serviceability was a great problem, although the new fighter quickly earned the respect of those Allied pilots who encountered it in combat. Nine prototypes and 998 production Shidens were built. The main variant was the N1K1-J Model 11 with the remarkably heavy armament of two fuselage-mounted 7.7mm Type 97 machine-guns, two wing-mounted 20mm Type 99 Model 2 cannons and two similar cannons in underwing gondolas.

Development of a modified version of the Shiden, Allied code name George, was planned in 1943 and the much-altered prototype N1K2-J first flew on 31 December that year. Even before service trials were completed production started and 423 aircraft were built, including eight prototypes. Shiden-Kai was a low-wing monoplane with an undercarriage of normal length. Fuselage and tailplane had been completely redesigned. The result was an extremely successful an popular intercepter and the N1K2-J was designated the standard land-based fighter and fighter-bomber, and widespread production was initiated at a large number of factories. In the event the American B29 bombing and the whole trend of the war prevented mass-production from getting under way.

It was on a Shiden-Kai that Japanese ace Warrant Officer Kinsuke Muto shot down four US Navy F6F Hellcats out of the dozen which had taken him on. Against enemy aircraft flying at low and medium altitudes the Shiden-Kai was very effective, but its performance at height was poor and it proved of limited value against B29s when they stepped up their systematic daylight raids on the homeland. Minor modifications were introduced and five later prototypes built, but the high-flying N1K5-J prototype was destroyed in an air raid before completion. The N1K2-J was armed with four wing 20mm Type 99 Model 2 cannons and served with the 201st, 341st,

Below: Kawasaki Army Ki45KAI prototype.

Below right: Kawasaki Army Type 2 of the 53rd Sentai, a home-defence unit as indicated by white-stripe background to the Hinomoru national marking.

343rd and Genzan Kokutais. Its top speed of 369mph (594km/h) at 18,375ft (5600m) and outstanding manoeuvrability won it great affection from its young Navy pilots.

The outstanding specialised night-fighter of the Japanese Navy Air Force was the Nakajima night fighter Gekko (Moonlight). The design stemmed from a 13-Shi (1938) requirement for a three-seat twin-engine long-range fighter. In the event, there were many problems, not least with the tandem remotely controlled dorsal machine-gun barbettes. The type finally appeared as the Type 2 reconnaissance aircraft (J1N1-C) and was given the Allied code name Irving.

Yasuna Kozono, commanding the 251st Kokutai at Rabaul in the New Hebrides, was getting weary of the apparent immunity of Consolidated B24 Liberator bombers during their nocturnal meanderings and under his direction a J1N1-C was modified by fixing two 20mm cannons in the observer's cockpit to fire obliquely forward at a 30-degree angle. Later, two downward-firing cannons were installed. Success came soon in the shape of two Liberators shot down at night. Soon the Navy ordered series production, the major modification being the elimination of the step between the rear of the observer's cockpit and the base of the vertical fin. Designated Gekko (J1N1-S), 183 were manufactured between April 1943 and March 1944 and another 240 before the last aircraft appeared in late 1944. Some machines had AI radar with external nose antennae and others had a small nose searchlight.

Other ingenious night-fighter adaptations included Kyokko, the Yokosuka P1Y2-S, developed from Frances, the P1Y1 bomber; the C6N1-S variant of Nakajima's reconnaissance aircraft Saiun, coded Myrt; and the D4Y2-S developed from the Yokosuka Suisei dive-bomber (Judy). None of them met with real success and few were put into service over Japan.

Several intercepter designs for the Navy failed to reach the production stage. Nakajima J5N1 Tenrai twin-engine prototypes were disappointing during 1944 tests, while the Aichi Denko S1A1 twin-engine night-fighter was destroyed during 1945 air raids. Production deliveries of the Mitsubishi Shusui (J8M1), based closely on the Me163B rocket fighter, had not started before the atom bombs were dropped. Perhaps the most promising type was the Kyushu J7W1 Shinden (Magnificent Lightning), a low-wing canard (tail-first) monoplane, which had horizontal control surfaces, with elevators attached to the nose, and aft-mounted swept-back wings with two vertical fins and rudders set part way along the trailing edge. The pilot's cockpit was located mid-way along the fuselage. The nose wheel retracted forward into the nose, the two rear mainwheels retracted inwards into the wings, while two auxiliary wheels retracted into the base of the vertical wing fins. A Mitsubishi 12 18-cylinder air-cooled radial engine rated at 2130hp for take-off drove a six-blade pusher propeller. Two prototypes were produced, the first flight taking place on 3 August 1945. A top speed of 466mph (750km/h) at 28,545ft (8700m) and climb to 26,245ft (8000m) were perhaps over-confident predictions, but the Shinden had the makings of a formidable weapon and perhaps it was fortunate for the American and British task forces preparing to invade Japan that no series aircraft had left the production lines when fighting ceased.

The Imperial Navy's fighter units had won great

acclaim in 1941 and 1942, acclaim based on the amazing impact of the Mitsubishi A6M Zero or Reisen. It brought renown to Japanese Navy fliers at home and created a myth among its many enemies. When the tide of war turned and the Zero was put on the defensive, exactly the reverse occurred. By then the Navy relied on largely inexperienced pilots, who found themselves up against odds in extremely unfavourable conditions. Their venerated Zero fighter, while marginally improved, had reached the end of its development potential and its inherent weaknesses were well known to its opponents, who by then were flying newer US fighters possessing what seemed unlimited potential. New Japanese fighter designs were a long time coming. The immediate successor to Zero was to be Reppu (A7M), but in fact it never came at all and against a total of about 11,000 Zero fighters of all versions, 1435 Shidens, 500 Raidens and just over 400 Gekko night-fighters were completed, an indication of the Navy's almost total reliance on a sole fighter type throughout nearly four years of bloody conflict.

The Koku Hombu or Army Air Headquarters made rapid strides with its fighter arm equipment throughout the Pacific War. Whereas the dependence on one single major design, at first a great asset, but later an

equally heavy liability, was the main feature of Japanese wartime naval fighter aviation, the Army introduced no fewer than five widely differing designs immediately prior to and during the four years of war in the Far East.

When Japan attacked, however, the vast bulk of the Army's fighter sentais and independent chutais were still equipped with the nimble Nakajima Type 97 fighter (Ki27); it was popular with its pilots, but underpowered for 1942 with a 650hp Type 97 radial engine giving 292mph (470km/h) at 11,480ft (3500m), and underarmed, with just two light machine guns. Yet even the Type 97 had its early successes against a demoralised enemy. Its pilots knew how to get the best from an aircraft which had first flown five years before Pearl Harbour and had been in service since 1937. Apart from the Type 97, code-named Nate under the Allied Pacific system, other fighter types equipped just three of the sentais committed to the conflict. There were two sentais of the Nakajima Type 1 fighter and a testing sentai equipped with the same firm's Type 2 intercepter.

The Nakajima Type 1 fighter Hayabusa (Peregrine Falcon) stemmed from a December 1937 instruction from the Koku Hombu. Hideo Itokawa's Ki43 prototype first flew from Ojima in January 1939. Two further prototypes and 10 pre-production aircraft followed and service trials lasted from November 1939 to September 1940. The influential instructors from the Akeno flying school complained from the outset that the Ki43 lacked the manoeuvrability of its predecessor, but it had been the same story when the Type 97 (Nate) had superseded the Kawasaki Type 95 biplane (Ki10) in the fighter sentais. From the eighth pre-production Hayabusa butterfly combat flaps were fitted, rendering the controls more sensitive and giving a really tight turning circle. The ninth pre-production machine had redesigned tail surfaces, a smaller-diameter fuselage and a 1100hp Nakajima Ha105 radial instead of the 950hp Ha25. The resulting aircraft even satisfied the Akeno school instructors!

The definitive aircraft spanned 37ft 6$\frac{1}{3}$in (11.44m) and weighed 4515lb (2048kg) loaded. Production was initiated and 40 Model 1As were delivered to the 59th and 64th sentais in China prior to December 1941. Production tempo increased and by mid-1942 the Hayabusa had replaced the Type 97 in many of the fighter chutais confronting the British, Australians and Americans in South-East Asia. There was no protection for pilot or fuel tanks and the Model 1A had just two 7.7mm Type 89 light machine-guns, one being replaced by a 12.7mm Type 1 weapon in the Model 1B. The Model 2A, produced from November 1942, had 13mm head and back armour for the pilot and rather primitive self-sealing fuel tanks. Models 1C and 2A had two 12.7mm guns and carried two 551lb (250kg) bombs in the fighter-bomber role.

As with the Zero, the Type 1's manoeuvrability took Allied pilots by surprise early in the war. A true pilot's aircraft, excellent in the stall and tight turn, it was soon outclassed in speed by its adversaries. When mastered, its vulnerability became evident. Model 1A had a speed of 308mph (495km/h) at 13,125ft (4000m) and could climb to 16,405ft (5000m) in five

Nakajima Ki44 first prototype with the manufacturer's test pilot at the cockpit.

minutes 30 seconds. With an 1150hp Ha1 15-I engine and three-blade constant-pitch airscrew, the Model 2 reached 329mph (530km/h) at 13,125ft (4000m) and the Model 3A had the Ha115-II of 1230hp giving 358mph (567 km/h) at 21,920ft (6680m). Altogether 5919 Hayabusas were built, including 716 Model 1s and 5170 Models 2 and 3 together.

Oscar, as it was known to the Allies, flew in every war theatre where the Japanese Army was engaged. Early on it served as an intercepter, throughout the conflict it was used for escort duties and from 1943 onwards it operated as a fighter-bomber. Surviving aircraft were expended in suicide attacks against ships of the US and British Pacific fleets.

In early 1938 the Nakajima company had been instructed to produce a high-speed intercepter, capable of reaching 373mph (600km/h) and climbing to 13,125ft (4000m) in no more than five minutes. It was a totally new concept for Nakajima and the Koku Hombu, for all previous emphasis had been on manoeuvrability and light wing-loading rather than speed. The first prototype Ki44 flew in August 1940. Designer T Koyama was disappointed at the 342mph (550km/h) attained at heavy expense — high wing loading and a landing speed which incurred the displeasure of Army test pilots.

Nine further prototypes and pre-production aircraft appeared during 1941 and considerable redesign took place. Trials with the 47th Independent Fighter Chutai in China from May to September 1942 were successful and improved maximum speed was registered. The Ki44 was then accepted as the Type 2 single-seat fighter Shoki (Demon) and 1225 were to be built up to the end of 1944. The principal production version was the Model 2, of which 1175 appeared from August 1942 onwards. The 1250hp Nakajima Ha41 engine of the Model 1 was replaced by the 1450hp Ha109. Most Model 2s were armed with four 12.7mm Type 1 machine guns, two in the fuselage and two in the wings. Wingspan of the Tojo, as the Type 2 was known to the Allies, was 31ft (9.45m) and wing area was 161.5sq ft (15m^2), compared with 35ft 6in (10.84m) and 230.4sq ft (21.4m^2) for the Type 1 Oscar. Top speed for the Type 2 Model 2B was 376mph (605km/h) at 17,060ft (5200m) and climb to 16,405ft (5000m) took four minutes 17 seconds, an

Above: Kawasaki Army Type 3 Model 1 Swallow, one of 388 Type 3s fitted with Mauser cannons instead of Japanese machine-guns.

Above right: Nakajima Army Type 2 Model 2A Demon intercepter warming up.

excellent performance by any standard.

The most famous unit flying the Type 2 was the 87th Sentai transferred from Manchuria (guarding against the Russians) to Sumatra in the Dutch East Indies to protect the vital oilfields there. The commanding officer of the 87th was Captain Hideaki Inayama, who achieved a high score of kills. When the situation in Sumatra became untenable, the 87th Sentai was withdrawn for home defence duties. The type met with far less success in defending Japan against US bombers, since it lacked the high-altitude capability to cope with the Boeing B29.

Following European trends, an Army specification for a twin-engine fighter was issued in March 1937. Rival projects were abandoned after a brief interval, leaving Kawasaki to follow a long and lonely development trail. An October 1937 Ki38 liquid-cooled engine mock-up was soon abandoned and then just two months later Kawasaki was instructed to work on the Ki45 specification. The prototype, designed by Takao Doi, appeared in January 1939, powered by two Ha20b 820hp radials. Most faults had been eliminated in the third prototype when completion of six pre-production aircraft was halted in late 1939. In April 1940 new Ha25 14-cylinder radials were fitted to one of the uncompleted airframes. The redesigned Ki45 KAI prototype appeared in May 1941. Three prototypes and 12 pre-production aircraft were tested successfully. Characteristics were a slim fuselage, increased wing span and generally an emphasis on simple straight contours with an almost pointed nose and neatly rounded tips to the wings and tail surfaces.

Production of the Type 2 twin-engine fighter Toryu (Dragon Slayer) started towards the end of 1941, and totalled 1701 of all versions. Span was 49ft 3½in (15.02m) and wing area was 344.4sq ft (32m²). the KA1a version reached 340mph (547km/h) at 22,965ft (7000m) and had a range of 1404 miles (2260km). Armament comprised two forward-firing fixed 12.7mm Type 1 machine-guns and a 20mm Ho3 cannon in a ventral tunnel and a flexible 7.92mm Type 98 machine-gun for the observer. The first Toryus to see combat went to the 16th Sentai in China and the 21st Sentai in Burma late in 1942. Coded Nick by the Allies, Toryu had good protection for crew and for fuel tanks. It was effective against Allied ground units and shipping.

The specialised ground-attack KAIb had a centrally mounted nose 20mm cannon and a hand-loaded 37mm cannon in a ventral tunnel. Most KAIb aircraft had the more-powerful Ha102 engines, a powerplant retained by the specialised night-fighter KAIc, which was armed with a semi-automatic 30mm Ho203

Nakajima Army Type 4 Model 1 Gale of the 11th Sentai.

ventral cannon and two 20mm Ho5 cannons mounted in the top fuselage decking to fire forward and upward at a 30-degree angle. The KAIc night-fighters had some success against B29s flying over Japan at night at low and medium altitudes. On one night early in their operational career they destroyed eight B29s.

During 1943 the Messerschmitt Bf109E fighter was reported in use by the Japanese. It had actually been tested by the Imperial Army, which had preferred the Kawasaki Ki61 and this aircraft, by then in service and designated the Type 3 fighter Hien (Swallow), was the formidable adversary which had been encountered. Kawasaki, strongly influenced by the past services of Richard Vogt (later of Blohm & Voss) as chief designer, had started to negotiate for the licence-manufacture of the Daimler-Benz DB601A inline engine as the Ha40. Two Ha40-powered projects were developed with Army encouragement, the Ki60, of which three examples were built, and the lighter Ki61. From December 1940 work was concentrated exclusively on the Ki61 by designers Takeo Doi and Shin Owada. The Ki61 employed a high-aspect-ratio wing of considerable area. Flight testing began in December 1941, by which time production lines had already been established. Twelve prototype and pre-production aircraft achieved speeds of up to 367mph (591km/h) at 19,685ft (6000m) and the Bf109E, the Russian LaGG3, the P40E, Ki43 and Ki44 were all outclassed in comparative trials.

The Type 3 was accepted early in 1942 and 2803 of all versions were built. The Model Ib had a wing span of 39ft 4in (12m) and wing area of 215.3sq ft (20m²). Its top speed was 368mph (592km/h) at 15,945ft (4860m) and it climbed to 16,405ft (5000m) in five minutes 31 seconds. Hien, Allied code name Tony, had high wing loading, achieved excellent speed in a dive, and set a new and welcome standard of pilot protection and self-sealing fuel tanks for Japanese Army fighters. Early aircraft had two fuselage 12.7mm Type 1 machine guns and two 7.7mm Type 89 wing guns, while later versions had four 12.7mm guns or two 12.7mm guns plus two 20mm Ho5 cannons. There were other even more heavily armed variants, of which the Ki61-I KAI and II KAI had underwing racks fitted for two 551lb (250kg) bombs.

While its engine remained troublesome and servicing difficulties reduced combat availability, the Hien nevertheless achieved a considerable reputation with friend and foe alike. Earlier operations over New Guinea underlined the need for easier maintenance and repair and for a strengthening of the structure to withstand fast diving speeds. The Ki61-I KAIc which went into production in January 1944 met these requirements at the expense of a higher all-up weight and slightly reduced performance. The Hien also saw service over Rabaul and later Okinawa, but it appeared in greatest numbers during the American invasion of the Philippines with the 17th, 18th and 19th Sentais, and finally in the defence of the homeland, operating with a total of seven sentais. The 244th Sentai, based in the Tokyo defence area and commanded by ex-bomber pilot Major Kobayashi, had a leavening of experienced pilots and did well against the Superfortresses and later against the US Navy's Hellcats and Corsairs, only meeting its master in the redoubtable P51 Mustang.

New versions, the Ki61-II and Ki61-II KAI, were powered by the 1500hp Ha140 engine, but only 129 had been completed when the Akashi engine plant was destroyed by bombing; 271 Hien airframes were left without powerplants. Urgent redesign and considerable ingenuity produced the Type 5 fighter, the Ki100-Ia, in reality the Ki61-II KAI airframe wedded to the Mitsubishi Ha112-II 14-cylinder double-row radial. The resulting aircraft was lighter than its predecessor and more manoeuvrable. Frontal drag naturally reduced speed, but the engine was more reliable and resulted in better serviceability. The Ki110-Ib, with all-round-vision canopy, was put into production and 121 were completed by the time of the Japanese surrender. The Type 5 maintained a respectable record, flown by the 5th, 17th, 59th, 111th and 244th Sentais.

The Nakajima Ki84 design was initiated to replace the Type 1 Hayabusa early in 1942. The first prototype, in March 1943, fulfilled the official requirement for an all-purpose long-range fighter capable of operating at combat rating for 1½ hours 250 miles from its base and of attaining a top speed of 423mph (680km/h). T Koyama and his team got the first prototype into the air in April and the second in June 1943, both powered by the 1900hp Ha45 18-cylinder engine. Then came 83 service trials and 42 pre-production aircraft. An experimental unit tested the new fighter in China under operational conditions. Redesignated the 22nd Sentai and commanded by Major Iwashi, it achieved considerable success against the US 14th Air Force. Ten sentais of Ki84s, by then designated the Type 4 fighter Hayate (Gale), were engaged in the desperate defence of the Philippines in 1944.

Production standards had fallen badly and undercarriage collapses and fuel system failures caused problems. Nevertheless a creditable 3509 Hayates had been completed by the war's end. The Ki84-I reached a maximum speed of 392mph (631km/h) at 20,080ft (6120m). Normal range was a respectable 1053 miles (1695km) and service ceiling was 34,450ft (10,500m). Loaded weight of 7995lb (3613kg) represented an almost 80 per cent increase over the Ki43 Hayabusa.

The Hayate, known to the Allies as Frank, was the best Japanese fighter to see large-scale service during the last year of war. It was effectively protected, fast and manoeuvrable. Treated with great respect by US pilots, it was prominent in all fighting areas from 1944 onwards.

The fuselage was a light-alloy structure built up from three sections, oval in form, and the wing was an all-metal single-spar structure. Fuselage, wings and tail unit all had light-alloy stressed-skin covering, except for the fabric-covered movable control surfaces. The mainwheels and tailwheel were hydraulically operated and fully retractable. The cockpit had a 65mm windscreen and 13mm head and back armour plate for the pilot. In the Model 2 the rear fuselage section was of wood. Various experimental developments included the Ki106 of all wood construction.

The only other Army fighters built in any numbers were the Mitsubishi Ki109 and Kawasaki Ki102. The Ki109 was adapted from the Type 4 heavy bomber and was originally conceived as a Ki109a/109b Superfortress hunter/killer combination. In 1944 22 Ki109s were modified to an aircraft intended to operate on its own, with a 75mm nose cannon and single defensive tail machine-gun, but they were ineffective.

There were 22 Ki102 heavy ground attack fighter prototypes and pre-production aircraft manufactured during 1944 and in October that year production was started of 215 Type 4 assault aircraft (Ki102b, coded Randy by the Allies). Six of the pre-production aircraft were modified from June 1944 as Ki102a high-altitude fighter prototypes, powered by two 1500hp Ha112-II Ru engines with Ru102 turbochargers, and armed with two Ho5 cannons and a single 37mm Ho203 cannon. Of 20 production Ki102b aircraft modified as pre-series Ki102a fighters only 15 had been delivered before the end of the war. A Ki102c night-fighter development with a longer fuselage, new cockpit, redesigned tail surfaces and wing of increased span and area, was built in prototype form only. The first aircraft flew in July 1945 and the second appeared in August. Intercept radar was to be carried and armament was to be two 30mm Ho105 belly cannons and two 20mm Ho5 cannons mounted obliquely aft of the cockpit.

Seven experimental fighter designs reached the prototype stage during 1941-1945, without going into production. Kawasaki produced two new single-seaters during 1943, three prototypes of the heavy Ki96 twin-engine fighter and a single example of the Ki64 high-speed fighter, powered by an Ha201 engine, in reality a pair of Ha40 engines in tandem — one in front of and one behind the cockpit — driving a pair of contra-rotating airscrews through a long extension shaft. Emphasis was placed on high-altitude twin-engine types, the first of four two-seat Mitsubishi Ki83s appearing in October 1944 and the two Kawasaki Ki108 single-seaters in March and May 1945.

The Nakajima Ki87 high-altitude single-seater, powered by a single 2400hp Ha44 radial with externally mounted supercharger and armed with two 20mm and two 30mm cannons, was deemed capable of reaching 439mph at 36,090ft (706km/h at 11,000m). The sole prototype was tested in April 1945, the same month as the first of two Rikugan Army Arsenal Ki93 heavy ground attack fighters, which were powered by twin Ha214s, also of 2400hp each. Finally, the scheduled first flight of the Tatchikawa Ki94-II, with a single turbocharged Ha44 and pressurised cockpit never took place; Japan had surrendered three days previously.

While the Japanese Navy Air Force had been inspired by the vision of a great conflict across thousands of miles of ocean and involving long over-water flights, not only by bombers and reconnaissance aircraft, but also by single-seat Zeros utilising drop-tanks and displaying considerable navigational skills, the Japanese Army's fighter arm was in a totally different situation. While displaying a high degree of courage and showing a great regard for Japanese history and heraldry in their colourful sentai insignia, Army fighter pilots knew that their role was almost exclusively the support of the armies on the ground. The Army Air Force had for years been orientated towards a land war with the Soviet Union in the north, rather than to campaigns over thousands of miles in the tropical and subtropical climates of the Pacific and the south. That it performed so well and was able to bring into use new aircraft to achieve objectives unforeseen until just before the outbreak of war was indeed creditable. It is perhaps a little unfair that the achievements of Army fliers were so often overshadowed by the publicity given to their Navy compatriots.

Above: Nakajima Ki84 fighter with wing cannon faired over.

Above right: Kawasaki Army Type 1 Model 1B of the 5th Fighter Sentai assigned to the defence of Nagoya in 1945.

Right: Ki84 fighters and Ki115 'suicide attackers' under construction at Nakajima's Ota plant.

39

Air Cargo's incredible variety

SYDNEY VEALE

All pictures used in this feature were supplied through the author

AIR CARGO, now running at nearly 20,000 million tons a year and still growing, is an industry in its own right employing thousands of people and serving every industry and profession from heavy engineering to obscure branches of science. The items that make up this huge traffic weigh anything from a few grammes to many tons.

At first, the growth of goods traffic was disappointingly slow and not until large fast long-range aircraft came into use did shippers find substantial advantage from sending their goods by air. Earlier, air freighting was worthwhile only if shipment was urgent. Now, many classes of merchandise go by air as a matter of routine, rather as most long-distance letters are sent by air mail.

Most of the traffic is carried in aircraft that started life as airliners and were made suitable for freight work by having their floors strengthened and their doors widened — and in some instances having hoists installed to facilitate loading and unloading without the use of airport equipment. A recent development is the use of 'Combi' airliners which carry large numbers of passengers and a great weight of freight in separate compartments.

To cope with the expanding cargo traffic airports have had to build special terminals with road systems for the vehicles bringing in outward-bound consignments, and collecting those for final delivery. Had passengers and goods not been separated all would now be chaos.

In general, sending goods by air is fairly straightforward. The items have to be adequately protected against damage in transit; certain documents must be made out and sent with the goods, and Customs formalities must be observed if the goods are going abroad. But the authorities impose no more restraints than are necessary. However, for some kinds of cargo

Head of the 40ft King Kong model used to promote the recent film was one of the three sections flown to Europe by Air France Boeing 747F.

AIR FRANCE

there are detailed regulations which must be closely followed and if infringed carry heavy penalties. Two such classes are live animals and 'restricted articles', the latter term being applied to dangerous substances, mostly chemicals.

In the past, live animals — the term embraces all living creatures from elephants to microscopic bacteria — have sometimes suffered harm and even casualties on the journey, from ignorance of the animals' needs, or through mistakes and misunderstandings. The regulations are a carefully compiled set of rules which, properly applied, make repetitions of earlier mishaps and tragedies impossible. The regulations list about three hundred names of birds, animals, fish, insects and other creatures from the aardvark to the zebu. Sometimes the instructions relate to a single species, at others to groups of species whose needs are largely the same.

The regulations are drawn up and published by the International Air Transport Association, the air transport industry's representative organisation. To help those who must know and apply them sets of slides and a commentary are available; by their use the various procedures are presented visually and aurally and remove uncertainties. Here are a few of the recommendations and instructions.

To reduce flying time to a minimum the shortest possible route must be taken. Consignments must be loaded no earlier than necessary. If two airlines are

involved, arrangements must be made in advance of departure to ensure that no unnecessary delay takes place at the interchange airport. Care must be taken to avoid arrival at week-ends or on public holidays at airports which do not provide Customs or vetinary services on those days.

At a hot airport en route the cargo hold doors must be opened if the inside temperature reaches 70 degrees F (20 degrees C) or thereabouts. Should this prove ineffective, mobile air-conditioning equipment must be

Above left: Looking rather like an underground railway tunnel, the huge main cargo deck of a Lufthansa 747F showing roller conveyors and cargo lashing points.

Left: A Boeing 707 of Pakistan International Airways taking aboard an Africa-Europe safari car.

Above: A Flying Tiger Line Boeing 747 convertible with side cargo door rigged for cargo and carrying a set of four P&W J69D turbofan engines as fitted to the 747./*Boeing*

called in. Care must be taken to ensure that natural enemies are not placed near one another at any time; predator and prey can often detect each other's presence by sound or smell as well as by sight, and it is not enough to prevent the two from seeing one another. If radio-active materials are also being carried, even in another hold, the living animals must be stowed at a prescribed distance dictated by the degree of radiation.

Also covered are problems relating to the watering and feeding of live animals before and during flight. Many species, if fed and watered shortly before loading, can make the journey without further attention. Conversely, other species need food and drink at frequent intervals. Seed-eating birds, for instance, must have food available all the time, and enough light to see it. Baby chicks are no trouble; for the first 72 hours of life they require neither food nor water, and in that time they can be flown thousands of miles from their birthplace and be none the worse for it.

Staff are warned not to give the animals tit-bits, and not to allow others to do so. Scores of casualties have been caused through this well-intentioned but misguided act. Sometimes it is necessary to create a natural environment artificially, as is the case with the dainty hummingbird. The spout of this bird's feeding bottle has to be painted red to make it look like part of a flower.

Designs of cages and containers for live animals, and the methods and materials of construction, are given in great detail, and no shipper is left wondering if he has the right travelling accommodation for his consignment. In many instances, one type of cage or container is suitable for only one species or sub-species; in others, one type of cage or container will suit a number of species. One such group consists of badger, bear, bobcat, cheetah, cougar, coyote, dingo, fox, hyena, jackal, jaguar, leopard, lion, lynx, ocelot, panther, polar bear, puma, tiger, warthog, wild boar, wild cat, wild dog, wolverine and wolf. Sometimes, one type of cage will serve for a short journey, but be inadequate for a long trip.

A great many cages — the majority in fact — are padded, but even padding does not always provide full protection. Penguins have first to be placed inside a cloth bag which is tied round the bird's neck, so that it

can move its head and legs but not flap its flippers.

All cages and containers that have the space carry 'This way up' labels on all four sides to prevent their being stowed inverted or on their sides. Other labels bearing appropriate outlines are used to identify the occupants. Animals for laboratory work which have been injected with dangerous bacteria have warning labels on the outside of their cages; some have to travel in germ-proof filter bags and if fed on the journey become useless for the experiment for which they were intended.

Some animals are not good air travellers and can become restive when on board. The authorities discourage the use of drugs to quieten them, but if a drug is the only solution, its name (or type), the dosage, and the estimated effective period of sedation must be made known to all who have to handle the animal en route.

Shippers of live animals started using the airways more than 50 years ago and there can now be few species that have yet to make their debut as air travellers. One early traveller was a pig which was taken aloft to prove that a popular saying was a fallacy. But that particular animal flew long before any regulations for its well-being had been framed.

Above: Special arrangements necessary to carry dolphins by air include foam rubber-lined canvas cradles with slits for flippers, at least 3in clear space at head and tail, and occasional spraying to keep their skin moist./*KLM*

Right: A KLM aircraft specially rigged to carry live cattle. Cattle breeders were among the first to take advantage of the speed and convenience of air transport./*KLM*

Restricted Articles

Dangerous substances, when first accepted by the airlines, had a habit of proving difficult to contain. The vessels in which they were placed often had faults that allowed the contents to leak and cause damage to the aircraft, to other cargo and danger to the crew. On one occasion escaping fumes forced a cargoplane's crew to don oxygen masks and make an emergency landing at an airport many miles short of the intended destination. Leaks have also caused fires and explosions on board.

The restricted articles regulations cover a list of dangerous substances that fills 44 pages of the relevant handbook. The manufacture and testing of containers

D. B. V.D. ZEE
CATTLE-EXPORT
LEEUWARDEN (HOLLAND)

Lufthansa
Luft
D-ABIW
BOEING 727
555
620

Above left: A complete mobile home being loaded aboard a Pacific Western Airlines Hercules in Canada.

Left: Igloo-shaped containers designed to make the most of the space for cargo about to be put aboard a Lufthansa Boeing 727.

Above: Long heavy loads were sometimes sent by air even before the big modern jet made them commonplace, as shown in this 1962 picture of an urgent replacement ship's propeller shaft carried from the US to Hong Kong in a Flying Tiger Line Lockheed Constellation./*Flying Tiger Line*

Right: Standard containers 40ft × 8ft × 8ft up to 55,000lb in weight are handled on and off modern jet freighters by Northwest Orient's Cochran 755 loader./*Northwest Orient*

for all the substances are given clearly and fully, and as a result failures are now extremely rare. The nature of the risk presented by the different substances is made plain by the type of label on the container. This gives warnings in words and by symbols whose meaning needs no explanation.

These and the live animals regulations are constantly under review and periodically revised in the cause of airline safety, the interests of shippers, the welfare of handlers and the arrival, unharmed and intact, of the items shipped.

All the signs are that the growth of air cargo in both volume and variety will oblige IATA to continue revising its current regulations at frequent intervals and, from time to time, to introduce new ones and thus maintain its watchful role in an industry still undergoing sweeping and rapid change.

Above: Only very occasionally live cargo escapes, as in the case of this baby chick given VIP treatment on the flight deck of a Transavia-Holland aeroplane carrying several thousand companions from the Netherlands to Africa.

Above right: The way millions of day-old chicks normally travel demonstrated by a 100,000 shipment for Greece being loaded aboard a Vickers Vanguard at Manston, Kent.

Right: Horses frequently figure as air cargo today, between stables, to and from race meetings and for the bloodstock market; here part of a consignment going to join Malta's police force boards a BAC Britannia at Stansted, Essex.

ROSS CHICKS
AIR CARGO

LLOYD INTERNATI

TRANSAVIA
HOLLAND

TriStar
BBAH
British
airways

Above left: Loaders often achieve the seemingly impossible, with millimetres to spare; their skill was well demonstrated in tucking these pipes into a Boeing 707 freighter at Schiphol.

Left and right: Modern mechanised loading equipment can quickly handle a wide variety of boxes and bundles, as demonstrated by these two pictures of a British Airways TriStar and its assorted cargo./*British Airports Authority*

Above right: The only fishy thing about this strange aircraft is its name. Originally a Boeing Stratocruiser, the monstrous fuselage was designed to carry very bulky loads such as rocket components too big for conventional machines. Three were built and named *Pregnant Guppy, Super Guppy,* and *Mini Guppy* respectively.

SIKORSKY S-64
N6979R
SIKORSKY SKYCRANE

TRADEWINDS

Above left: Just another way of moving house, demonstrating the ability of the S64 Sikorsky Skycrane, designed originally as a military transport with interchangeable cargo pods as well as the 15,000lb hoist.

Left: Not pilgrims but aluminium extrusions bound for Mecca, Saudi Arabia, for highway balustrading, part of an export order won by High Duty Alloys, being loaded aboard a Tradewinds Canadair CL44 at London Gatwick Airport. */Hawker Siddeley Group*

Above: An electronic simulator designed and produced by Redifon Flight Simulation Ltd for the Boeing E3A AWACS airborne early warning station being loaded aboard a chartered Galaxy freighter at USAF Base Mildenhall, Suffolk, for shipment to America.

Right: Pallets awaiting loading aboard a Seaboard World 747F at London Airport typify the remarkable variety of airfreight today.*/British Airports Authority*

The avenging Grumman

JAMES GOULDING

All pictures used in this article were supplied by Philip J R Moyes

WHEN WAR BROKE OUT in September 1939 the standard torpedo-bomber of the US Navy was the Douglas TBD1 Devastator single-engine monoplane. This low-wing aircraft had proved to be a reliable and tractable torpedo-bomber, well liked by its crews and a pleasant flying machine. It was, however, lightly armed and with the added drag of an only partially stowed torpedo the aircraft was slow and clearly obsolescent as far as modern warfare was concerned. Plans were therefore put in hand to develop a more potent replacement, and to that end a contract was placed on 8 April 1940 with the Grumman Aircraft Engineering Corporation by the Bureau of Aeronautics. The contract called for the design, development and construction of a three-seat single-engine torpedo-bomber capable of operation from existing aircraft carriers, and the order covered construction of two prototypes under the designation of Grumman XTBF1.

The XTBF1 was a typical product of the Grumman Corporation's design team, with angular straight taper on wings, fin and rudder, and tailplane leading edge. Having a bomb bay deep enough to accommodate four 500lb bombs or one 22in torpedo totally enclosed by doors, below the wing, and space for a pilot, navigator/gunner and radio-operator/gunner in the compartment above the wing, the fuselage of the XTBF1 was portly. The crew compartment was covered by a massive glazed fairing culminating in a power-operated turret housing a single 0.5in gun mounted offset to port. An under-fuselage gun position, mounting a single 0.3in gun, protected the potential blind spot under the tail. A fixed 0.5in gun mounted in the starboard side of the top decking forward of the windscreen was aimed and fired by the pilot.

The American carrier USS *Enterprise* homeward bound off the Florida coast from the Pacific war in October 1945, with one of her Grumman Avengers flying overhead.

16
16
16

The new torpedo-bomber was powered by a single Wright R2600-8 two-row 18-cylinder air-cooled engine of 1700hp, which bestowed a top speed of 251mph at sea level and 271mph at 12,000ft. Normal cruising speed was 145mph and the range when carrying a 22in torpedo was 1215 miles. The XTBF1 had an all-metal structure with fabric-covered ailerons, elevators and rudder, and the outer main planes were designed to fold back for stowage aboard aircraft carriers. The undercarriage units were all retractable, the main legs folding outwards into the wings, with the wheels left exposed in their housing wells.

The first prototype of the new Grumman torpedo-bomber (BU Aer No 2539) was completed during the summer of 1941 and made its maiden flight on 1 August in the hands of test pilot Bob Hall. Test flying of the first XTBF1 by the company's pilots progressed satisfactorily; the only problem requiring rectification was some directional instability, which was improved on the second prototype by the addition of a fin extension. Test flying with the first aircraft continued until 28 November 1941, when a disastrous bomb-bay fire forced the two crew members to abandon the aircraft.

Three pictures featuring Grumman Avengers in service aboard USN aircraft carriers. The one on the left shows the early trials of the use of tractors to replace manual manoeuvring of aircraft aboard carriers.

Test flying of the new type was delayed until December, when the second aircraft was completed and flown around the 20th. In December an initial production order for 286 of the Grumman aircraft under the designation of TBF1 was given, although production had already got under way on the understanding that an order would be confirmed. The first production TBF1 joined the test programme on 3 January 1942 and was in most respects similar to the second prototype. This aircraft was taken on charge by the US Navy at the end of the month and such was the rate of production that 85 TBF1s had been completed by the end of May 1942, with a further 60 delivered to the US Navy a month later.

The Battle of Midway began on 4 June 1942 and it was there that the first TBF1s (by then named Avengers) were in action for the first time, flown by US Navy Squadron VT-8, which was in the process of being re-equipped with the new type in place of Devastators. The battle was disastrous for the American torpedo-bomber squadrons and VT-3, VT-6 and VT-8 lost 38 of a force of 42 Douglas TBD Devastators without damaging the enemy. During the action six TBF1 Avengers from VT-8, operating from Midway, attacked the Japanese fleet and only one, badly damaged, survived. The debacle recalled a similar debut in earlier times when four out of five Bristol F2B fighters were shot down on their first action against the enemy, but that British two-seater went on to establish itself as one of the truly great

combat aircraft of the 1914-18 war. So, too, did the Avenger, after such a grim start to its career, become established as one of the most successful US Navy aircraft.

Production of the Avenger continued at Grumman and 1525 Avengers were ordered, many being converted into variants of the basic type. To increase production of the type and permit Grumman to continue development of the Hellcat and subsequent

Below: A TBF1 from one of the early deliveries in mid-1942.

Bottom: A picture showing useful detail of the Avenger's clean undersurfaces.

Right: Picturesque and neat formation of TBF1Bs which were similar to the early delivery to the Royal Navy, originally to be named Tarpon.

Navy fighters, a contract was placed with the Eastern Division of General Motors to place the Avenger in production under the designation TBM. The first of them was the TBM1 in various versions, of which 2882 were built by the Eastern Division. The GM-built aircraft were similar to the TBF1 and were powered by the same engine, the Wright R2600-8 radial of 1700hp.

Grumman eventually stopped production of the TBF1 Avenger in December 1943, after completing a total of 2293; the variants were the TBF1, TBF1B, TBF1C, TBF1CP, TBF1D, TBF1E, TBF1J, TBF1L, TBF1P, XTBF2 and XTBF3. The TBF1 and TBF1C were the major production variants, the 1C having increased fuel tankage and two 0.5in guns in the wings (one in each wing) in place of the single gun mounted in the top decking. The TBF1B was the version supplied under Lease-Lend aid to the Royal Navy, 402 being delivered (FN750-FN949, JT773, JZ100-JZ300); they were known in the Royal Navy originally as Tarpon 1s, but eventually the name Avenger 1 was used.

The 21st production TBF1 was fitted with a Wright XR2600-10 engine and this experimental Avenger, which made its maiden flight on 1 May 1942, was designated XTBF2. The designation XTBF3 was given to two prototypes fitted with the Wright R2600-20 radial engine of 1900hp. This improved Avenger was not produced by Grumman in quantity, but the two aircraft were used to carry out the test programme for the Eastern-built TBM3.

As already related the first major production type built by Eastern was the TBM1, similar in all respects to the TBF1 and powered by the Wright R2600-8 1700hp engine. Subtypes of the TBM1 were the TBM1C, TBM1CP, TBM1E, TBM1J, TBM1L and TBM1P. Four prototypes of the XTBM3 joined the XTBF3s in the test programme for the second major Eastern-built production Avenger, the TBM3, of which no fewer than 4657 TBM3s and TBM3Es were built.

The Royal Navy received 334 TBM1Cs, known as Avenger Mk IIs, and 222 TBM3s and TBM3Es under

Above: Excellent detail revealed in an air-to-air shot of flights of Pacific Fleet Air Wing Avengers in 1947.

Above right: An ex-USN GM-built TBM3 converted experimentally in 1947 to a freighter using the one-time torpedo compartment for cargo.

Right: A US carrier's AA guns smoking after driving off a Japanese dive-bomber attack during the Leyte battles, in which carrier-based Avengers figured prominently.

EXPERIMENTAL
NX 41854

the designation Avenger Mk IIIs. A further order for TBM4s, 70 aircraft, did not materialise because this version did not in the end go into production. Three prototypes of the TBM4 were flown under the designation XTBM4 and featured improvements in wing construction and folding. The TBM4 was to have been built in quantity but the end of the Pacific war brought an end also to production plans.

Avengers took part with success in most of the great battles of the Pacific war in numerous roles. They were used for air support of ground forces, with rockets and bombs, and as dive-bombers, with armour-piercing bombs, and in the role for which they had been designed, torpedo-bombers, with 22in torpedos. In the anti-shipping role they sank many ships and they contributed to the sinking of the Japanese carriers, *Chitose, Chujoda, Zuiho Hiyo,* and *Zuikaku* and the two great battleships, *Musashi* and *Yamato,* the largest ever built. In the case of the two battleships Avengers scored 19 hits with torpedos on the *Musashi* and 10 against the *Yamato.*

The Royal Navy used Avengers in the anti-submarine role in the North Atlantic and in the anti-shipping role in support of the Allied landings during Operation Overlord. In the Far East the Avenger was effectively used by the Royal Navy as its major strike aircraft.

Above: Sharp shadows denote bright midday sun in this picture of an early TBF1; the rudder striping was dropped by the US Navy after 1942.

Above right: A British Fleet Air Arm pilot gets a hand to board his training Avenger at a US Navy air base.

Avengers continued to give excellent service during the post-war period, operating with the naval units of the US Navy and US Marine Corps, the Royal Navy, Royal Canadian Navy, French Aeronavale, Royal Netherlands Naval Air Service, the Servicio Aéronautica de la Marina of Uruguay and, ironically, by the Japanese Maritime Self Defence Force. In civil guise Avengers were modified for the role of fire-fighting.

The Avenger in scale

Over the years the Avenger has been the subject of numerous plastic kits in various scales, although now

about three are easily available. The largest models have been in 1:48 scale and produced by Lindberg and Monogram. The latter kit is readily available and is a fine replica of the TBF1. Moulded in dark blue, Monogram's model has a number of operating features which were characteristic of the full-size aircraft. The wings fold realistically and the bomb doors open to reveal the 22in torpedo. The large rear turret revolves and the gun elevates. The undercarriage retracts and the tailwheel is lowered by extending the 'sting' arrester hook. The external detail is excellent and typical of Monogram kits. The transfer (decal) sheet gives markings for a typical US Navy aircraft, although the unit is not specified.

The other easily obtainable kits are both in 1:72 scale and one by Airfix and Frog. Both kits are good representations of the TBM1. Of the two the Airfix kit is a little more detailed in respect of the engine, and has underwing rockets. External detail on the Frog model is in the form of delicate skin lines, with a few rivets around the engine cowling and wing roots, whereas the Airfix model has masses of rivets over the entire model, but fortunately they are not too heavy. An interesting point about the Frog model is that it seems to have been moulded internally to have motorisation at a later date (several Frog kits were reissued with electric motors).

The Airfix model has US Navy markings whereas the Frog model represents an Avenger MkII of either 857 Squadron with the British Pacific Fleet or when based at Macrihanish. Anyone wishing to model the Avenger is well served by any of these kits, with the Monogram kit providing splendid scope for super-detailing.

Avenger Colours

A wide variety of colour schemes was to be found on Avengers according to where, or by whom, they were operated. Perhaps the most numerous colour scheme was the standard US Navy scheme. In this the upper surfaces of the wings and tailplane were painted in semi-gloss sea blue and the upper surface of the fuselage was in non-specular (matt) sea blue. The sides of the fuelage and fins were non-specular intermediate blue, and the undersurfaces of the wings, tailplane and fuselage were non-specular white. The upper-surface leading edges of the wings and tailplane were in non-specular sea blue in contrast to the semi-gloss finish of the rest of the upper surfaces.

Some Avengers of the US Navy had non-specular

Above: Caught in the act with belly doors still open, a USN Avenger launches its 2000lb 22in torpedo.

Right: A flight of TBF1s from the original batch of 200 for the Royal Navy.

sea blue upper surfaces to the fuselage and semi-gloss sea blue on the wings and tailplane upper surfaces, with non-specular white on all under surfaces and in some cases up the fuselage sides and on the fin. In later years some US Navy, Royal Navy, Canadian Navy, Royal Netherlands Navy and French Aeronavale Avengers were painted overall in semi-gloss sea blue.

Avengers in wartime Royal Navy service were usually painted in the temperate sea scheme colours of extra dark sea grey and dark slate grey, with overall sky on the under surfaces. Some Royal Netherlands Navy Avengers were painted in extra dark sea grey overall on the upper surfaces and sky overall on the under surfaces. Royal Canadian Navy Avengers were often painted in extra dark sea grey overall on the upper surfaces an light grey overall on the under surfaces.

During the later post-war period the Royal New Zealand Air Force used Avengers for target-towing duties and they were either painted overall in black and yellow stripes or with overall aluminium on the upper surfaces and black and yellow stripes on the lower surfaces.

4D
4F

Above left and right: More of the first Lend-Lease batch, which were numbered FN750-949.

Left: A 1944 picture of a RN Avenger 1 showing wing folding.

Right: A Grumman Avenger AS4 at RNAS Culdrose in November 1958, one of a batch of ex-US Navy aircraft acquired by the Royal Navy.

ROYAL NAVY

380

Rust, restoration and resurrection

PHILIP BIRTLES

THE AIRCRAFT restoration movement is growing rapidly in many countries of the world, and particularly in Britain, with the increasing awareness of the historical value and interest in aviation. As more people find they can afford to fly, particularly on relatively inexpensive inclusive tours, the public are becoming more air minded. Aviation also makes news, although regretfully mainly when disaster strikes, but from time to time even good aviation news makes the headlines.

With the increasing numbers of aviation museums and collections in the UK, often run by gifted amateurs or underpaid enthusiasts, the average enthusiast finds he can actually become involved in aviation himself in a practical way. People with no formal training or experience can find themselves working with qualified engineers on restoring anything from a part of a wartime Spitfire dug up after over 30 years under the ground, to restoring a complete aircraft to flying condition. An example is a VHF selector box from a crashed Mosquito, buried for over 33 years in marshland in the Fens, restored recently to working order as good as when it was new. At the other extreme is the restoration to flying condition of the sole surviving de Havilland Comet Racer, G-ACSS, by the Shuttleworth Trust after about 40 years of inactivity.

Restoration of the Comet was once considered quite impossible by many experts, but on closer inspection the wooden airframe was found to be in remarkably good condition after all those years. It is often the metal aircraft which cause most problems for restoration; where serious corrosion has set in parts

The oldest de Havilland Rapide in existence, G-ADAH is loaned by the Aeroplane Collection to the Museum of Flight at East Fortune and is being restored and reassembled. It still carries its original markings of Allied Airways (Gandar Dower).
/G Watson, Aeroplane Collection

ALLIED AIRWAYS
(GANDAR DOWER) LTD
Pioneer

Two pictures of the ex-Portuguese Air Force Junkers Ju52/3m 6316, above, en route to Duxford by road for preservation, and the completed aircraft painted in Luftwaffe markings nearly three years after it arrived./*Philip J Birtles*

can either be impossible or very expensive to replace. In fact in aircraft restoration nothing is really impossible, but engines cause the biggest problems because of their special materials, tighter tolerances, difficulty with replacement parts and general wear and tear.

Most of the museums and aviation collections undertake some form of preservation and restoration of their exhibits, although the initial problems are locating, acquiring, recovering and transporting exhibits to a suitable home.

In the case of recovery, if the remains of an aircraft crash are not on the surface a considerable effort has to be made carefully to excavate the site. Before starting work however, permission must be obtained not only from the landowner, but the Ministry of Defence and the local police. Many of the buried wrecks still have highly dangerous unexploded bombs and ammunition around them; there could also be the remains of crew members still on board and it is essential that they should be dealt with correctly. Often a service liaison officer can be seconded to a recovery group and can be extremely helpful in clearing any official snags involved in a dig. It is also essential to tidy up the site when the excavation has been completed otherwise it might not be so easy to persuade another landowner to agree to a dig on his land.

Another fairly common form of wreck recovery is from remote crash sites where aircraft have hit high ground. Some are so remote that it is practically impossible for many of the parts to be salvaged, except for the smaller bits and pieces. Many of the largest pieces of wreckage, including broken engines, lie scattered over the hills slowly corroding away, as a memorial to their gallant crews. Surprisingly, some wrecks have actually provided a source of much-needed spare parts, especially engine components, helping to keep other rare vintage aircraft in the air.

In an attempt to fill in the gaps caused by the neglect to preserve many historic aircraft in the past a highly specialised form of recovery which has been developing recently is the raising of aircraft from under water. The most successful of these types of recovery is from fresh water, the most popular area being the Scandinavian lakes. Gloster Gladiators and even a Handley Page Halifax have been recovered so far and, although they will obviously never fly again, their condition is generally remarkable apart from any precrash and impact damage. Unfortunately, when such wrecks have been well known, they have sometimes been vandalised during prior visits by skin

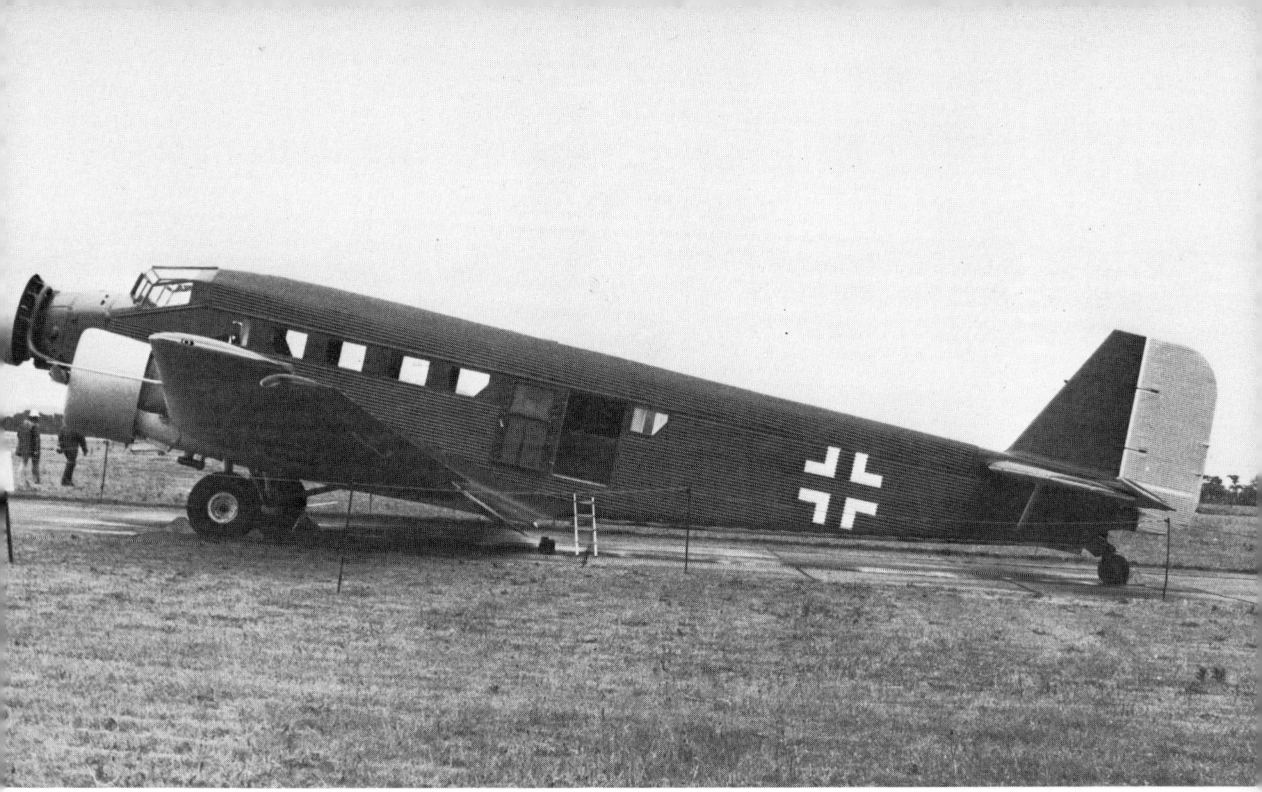

divers who are less interested in aircraft preservation.

Even wrecks which have been recovered from salt water can provide enough castings, forgings and so on capable of being cleaned up, and the remains of the sheet metal can be used as patterns to reconstruct what in effect becomes a non-flying replica. Work started some time ago at Duxford on an Me109 salvaged from the water in Norway; an He111 was collected at the same time. Although some areas of the wreck have been destroyed by fire and later corrosion, other parts are in remarkably good condition and complete with their original paint.

After finding a crash site, one attraction with the recovery of wrecks is the detective work involved in identifying the original aircraft type, its serial number, its service unit and why it crashed. Many of the wrecks dug up after many years have been surprisingly well preserved after their long immersion, as far down as 30 feet, in clay. The engines in particular appear to survive well, usually surrounded in their own engine oil, and can be a useful source of parts to keep some rare aircraft flying.

The majority of museums however thrive on the complete aircraft they have managed to obtain. Some have exhibits going back to the early days of aviation, while others have a comparatively recent collection, taking advantage of a more enlightened time in the preservation of our aeronautical heritage. Few aircraft types are now allowed to vanish into obscurity and others are revived from a few parts to a shining example of a near replica, using the original rotting wood and rusty metal as a guide in the restoration.

There is a perennial argument about whether a restored aircraft should be allowed to fly or not. The purists say that if an aircraft is preserved it should be allowed to fly and be seen in the air, otherwise it is a lifeless exhibit. Others say that a unique aircraft, preserved and restored with great care, should not be risked in the air, in case it should crash and be destroyed. There are, of course, examples of that happening in the past. While some museums do not allow their own aircraft to fly, they will gladly help to keep others flying by swopping good engines for life-expired ones and lend equipment to make a restored aircraft more authentic.

There are other organisations who not only do not allow their aircraft to fly but will not allow engines to be run, or other exhibits to work, in case deterioration is caused by wear and tear. For the smaller collections the question of whether to fly or not is answered quite simply by the level of finance and qualified people available to help. It is also easier to contemplate operating a historic aircraft if it has arrived at the museum in flying condition and steps are taken to keep it in working order from the start, unless of course it is a V-bomber and then there is probably little point in hoping to fly such an aircraft again. Still, who would have thought a few years ago that anyone would want to preserve a Varsity, and now at least two are flying regularly in Britain.

The ultimate of course is the restoration of an aircraft to full flying condition, restored accurately to represent an earlier period in its life. There are various ways in which this can be achieved from a no-expense-spared commercial restoration for a film company to the modest back-garden shed of a group of amateurs.

Perhaps one of the major screen epics of recent years was the Battle of Britain film, for which a number of Spitfires and a Hurricane were brought back to airworthiness standard, while others were restored to taxying condition. The Spanish Air Force supplied the Me109s and He111s, although they were powered by Rolls-Royce Merlins. Such is the value of these old aircraft nowadays that crash sequences were simulated with flying models and full-scale wooden replicas. As a result of the restoration work done for the film several Spitfires are now flying regularly, having been kept in good condition, including a MkII with the RAF Historic Flight and the Mk Vc restored at Duxford for the Shuttleworth Trust by a dedicated group of volunteers.

The Duxford group worked many hours of their own time to complete this fine restoration and their labours are amply rewarded when the aircraft is seen flying in completely authentic markings. They are now continuing to use their skills and experience to restore a Spitfire PRXI, which has been on static display at Old Warden in the open for many years, and which is expected to fly again, and so is an Anson which was

Above: The last known Halifax bomber recovered from under water in Lake Hoklingen in Norway for restoration by the RAF Museum.

Above right: Anson C19 TX183, last used by A & AEE Boscombe Down, stripped down for restoration./*Philip J Birtles*

Right: The Shuttleworth Trust Spitfire Vc AR501 beautifully restored to flying condition in the colours of 310 (Czech) Sqn./*Philip J Birtles*

AR501
DNN

T
WP790

T

Above left: The stripped fuselage of Chipmunk WP790 ready for removal to the Mosquito Aircraft Museum in December 1974. */Philip J Birtles*

Left: Trying the wings on Chipmunk WP790 after restoration of the fuselage and tail was completed.*/Philip J Birtles*

Above: Chipmunk WP790 in the colours of Birmingham University Air Squadron at Benson in September 1970. It will be restored to this standard.*/Philip J Birtles*

parked next to it. The fabric covering of the Anson has naturally deteriorated much more than the metal Spitfire.

Other work at Duxford includes the restoration to static condition of a P51 Mustang and an ex-Portuguese Air Force Junkers Ju52/3m in the colours of the German Desert Air Force, and work is starting on a B17 Flying Fortress and Short Sunderland flying-boat recently recovered from France. As the policy of the Imperial War Museum, part of whose collection is housed at Duxford, is not to fly its aircraft, none of those mentioned are restored to flying condition, but with such large aircraft, all of which are in relatively poor condition, it would probably be impractical to consider anyway.

The RAF Museum also has the rule that none of its aircraft will be flown again, although in many cases they have been donated in airworthy condition, or during their restoration they have been returned to, or very close to, working order. Much of the restoration of the RAF Museum exhibits has been undertaken by a group of highly skilled senior RAF technicians while serving out their last years before retirment from the service. They bring with them the skills of an earlier age and undertake a wide variety of work, preparing many of the aircraft and other exhibits at Hendon and continuing the restoration of what are often derelict exhibits held in store at Henlow and Cardington.

These highly skilled tradesmen obviously cannot cope with the volume of work involved and their efforts are supplemented by the work of many volunteers, both RAF and civilian, at a number of establishments around the country. Perhaps the major RAF unit which has prepared aircraft for the RAF Museum is St Athan, where a group of volunteers restore and maintain a fine collection of German World War II aircraft, as well as a number of other types. No 5 Maintenance Unit at RAF Kemble also carries out the major overhauls and repainting of the Lancaster, Spitfires and Hurricanes of the Historic Flight. The RAF Museum is supplemented by its regional reserve collections at Cosford and Finningley in addition to St Athan, and is planning to make use of Biggin Hill also.

Another fine Service museum, expanding rapidly and strongly supported, is the Fleet Air Arm Museum at Royal Naval Air Station Yeovilton. A fine collection of aircraft tracing the history of the Fleet

Air Arm has been assembled there, and in some cases a reserve aircraft is also available. The policy of the FAA Museum is to fly some exhibits where possible and at the time of writing two Sea Furies, a Firefly, a Swordfish and a Tiger Moth are available to travel around the air displays in the summer season, delighting the crowds. Although the Firefly seems to be troubled by technical snags and the Sea Fury was damaged in a landing accident (it has since been repaired) the flying museum aircraft do a fine job in promoting the Royal Navy. There appears to be little reason why some of the other aircraft in the museum should not fly again, the Sea Hawk for example, and groups of enthusiasts in the Fleet Air Arm continue to restore exhibits from the most derelict parts. Other aircraft have been restored in the past as exercises in RN training establishments, one of the best examples being a Supermarine Walrus.

One of the best known and oldest collections of preserved transport vehicles is the Shuttleworth Trust at Old Warden, where cars and bicycles are preserved in addition to aircraft. The aim of the Shuttleworth Trust, which is a registered educational charity, is to have all its exhibits in working order. There is a fine collection of aircraft, from a Blackburn Monoplane to the Jet Provost prototype G-AOBU, although the latter is not currently airworthy. Many of the collection are featured at the flying days throughout the summer season and the workshops are not only busy maintaining the existing aircraft, but work on major restoration projects; examples are a Hawker Hind recovered from Afghanistan and the 1934 London to Melbourne Air Race winner, the de Havilland Comet Racer.

The Afghan Hind was recovered after many years stored in the open and despite a fair amount of corrosion in much of the structure, it will eventually be restored to flying condition. The Comet Racer is one of the largest and most expensive restorations undertaken by the Shuttleworth Trust. Before work could be started an appeal for money had to be launched and a great deal of preliminary research work had to be done on the detail design, as only an empty shell remained. Drawings and information have been unearthed and where not available new drawings have been made. After many years in the open, followed by a rough and ready restoration for the Festival of Britain in 1951, and then display in the

Three pictures of Strathallan's Miles Magister G-AHUJ, loaded for delivery in February 1975, the restored fuselage before painting and on air test in military marking R1914 when it flew on 26 June 1976.

heated engine showroom at Rolls-Royce Leavesden, the condition of the structure was certainly suspect.

However, much to everyone's surprise, when it was dismantled only minor repairs needed to be made to the fuselage undersides, and on removal of the lower wing skin, the structure was found to be in excellent condition, thanks to the high quality of the original manufacture. In addition to the airframe work being done by the employees at Old Warden, the engines are being overhauled by Hants and Sussex Aviation, and other work is being done by other companies, including a fair contribution by Hawker Siddeley Aviation at Hatfield and Chester.

While the Shuttleworth Trust employees are busy keeping the aircraft maintained at Old Warden other groups of volunteer enthusiasts rebuild selected aircraft around the country; recent examples are the DH51 and a Hornet Moth at the HSA factory at Chester, and a DH53, first restored at Hatfield and then rebuilt after one of its crashes by the Army at Aborfield. More recently work on a Hurricane has been shared out between Staverton and Heathrow, where it will be restored to the flying condition deemed impossible when it was considered for the Battle of Britain film.

One of the more remote aircraft museums is the varied and rapidly growing Strathallan Aircraft Collection in Scotland, where aircraft in all conditions have been collected from far and wide, many to be eventually rebuilt to flying condition. Among the rarer

Shuttleworth Trust's Hawker Hind from Afghanistan, as it arrived at Old Warden in spring 1971 and, right, with fuselage inverted in May 1975, well on the way to completion of the very extensive rebuild./*Air Portraits*

and most difficult tasks are the rebuilding of a Westland Lysander, a Bristol Bolingbroke and a Fairey Battle, but the recovery from Canada of an Avro Lancaster and from Australia a Lockheed Hudson were perhaps most surprising. Although aircraft such as the retired Comet 2R, which was damaged on landing at Strathallan, and the Vampire T11 are unlikely to fly again, a Hurricane, Mosquito, Harvard, Spitfire and others have been fully restored.

Among the many other museums and collections around the country it is difficult to single out any one as they all do an excellent job in providing an outlet for the enthusiasm of the devotees, and in educating the public. Some collections are still trying to find permanent sites, others are more fortunate in having a nearby airport prepared to share some of its space and the most fortunate manage to acquire suitable land. Aircraft preservation is not discouraged even where no permanent home exists as exhibits can be loaned to other museums where they can be appreciated. The Aeroplane Collection is probably the best example of this category, although it is one of the oldest organisations in the preservation movement. On the other hand, the Midland Aircraft Preservation Society has recently moved out of the no-fixed-abode stage and is in the process of establishing the Midland Air Museum at Coventry Airport.

Among the longer established smaller museums are the Historic Aircraft Museum at Southend; the Lincolnshire Aviation Museum, which uses the unlikely site of the Old Station Yard at Tattershall; the Mosquito Aircraft Museum, which complements the adjacent privately owned mini-stately home where the Mosquito was designed; the Newark Air Museum on the disused Winthorpe Airfield now used as the county show ground; the Skyfame Museum at Staverton

Above: The stripped fuselage of the Spitfire PR11 at Duxford in June 1976 during its major rebuild to flying condition after many years in the open at Old Warden./*Air Portraits*

Right: RAF Museum's Hawker P1127 XP831, first of the HS Harrier V/STOL fighter's precursors to achieve transition from vertical to horizontal flight in September 1961./*Stuart Howe*

Next page: Torbay Aircraft Museum's beautifully preserved BA Swallow 2./*Mike Jerram*

AERO
FLIGHT
1961

G-AFGE

FB
Y

Above left: Hull of the Supermarine Seagull V VH-ALB while in the workshop at RAF Museum, Hendon./*Stuart Howe*

Left: Privately owned Spitfire 16 TB863 receiving attention in the Duxford workshops./*David Kingston*

Above: Early stages in the restoration by the Strathallan Collection of Westland Lysander III G-AZWT. /*Strathallan Collection*

Airport; and the Torbay Aircraft Museum on a tree-lined hilltop site in Devon.

Collections of more recent origin are the Cornwall Aeronautical Park near Culdrose, the North East Vintage and Veteran Aircraft Association, the South Wales HAPS forming at Cardiff Airport, the Thorpe Water Park at Egham in Surrey, the growing Rotorcraft Collection at Weston-Super-Mare and the Warbirds Museum at Blackbushe.

Most collections have a band of enthusiasts working in their spare time to make the exhibits more presentable and in some cases they house airworthy aircraft; even some of those not restored to fly can at least be taxied, an example being the Firefly at Staverton. There was a time when both the Skyfame Anson and Oxford were flown, but expense makes this a rare occurrence these days. Some groups specialise in a particular area of aviation; the Rotorcraft museum is the obvious helicopter collection, the Mosquito Aircraft Museum specialises mainly in the products of the de Havilland companies, Newark Air Museum tends to sponsor aircraft from its surrounding area and the Cornwall and Thorpe collections are Fleet Air Arm orientated. Perhaps Thorpe is best known for the flying Supermarine S5 racing seaplane replica, but there is also a Tiger Moth on floats in flying condition.

Another notable Supermarine aeroplane is the S6 of Schneider Trophy fame preserved with a Spitfire in the Mitchell Museum at Southampton, where a point of interest is not so much the restoration of the aircraft but the establishment of a suitable home by adapting

Left: The derelict fuselage of the Supermarine Walrus Mk1 2301 as it was found at Thame in Oxfordshire in 1963, and the fully restored Walrus after nearly three years' work by the RN Engineering School at Arbroath. It is now preserved at Yeovilton./*Both Fleet Air Arm Museum*

Right: The Airspeed Horsa glider cockpit after lying derelict for about 27 years, awaiting start of restoration./*Hawker Siddeley*

an old dance hall. Something that the public does not in general appreciate is the huge problem of getting shelter for the aircraft; when left outside in all weathers it is practically impossible to complete a restoration since fabric, dope, paint and so on all need to be applied in carefully controlled conditions to achieve success. To obtain even a modest agricultural building for shelter usually needs £10,000 or more. No amateur museum can earn that sort of money from entry charges, so resort has to be made to appeals and fund-raising activities to try and win the battle with the elements.

It is also difficult to mix a public viewing area with the necessary working areas, although the public apparently always likes to view what goes on in the workshops. When workshop visits are permitted the work areas must be kept clean and tidy and be constantly manned to answer questions and keep a watchful eye on the exhibits; also ways must be found to allow visitors to see what goes on without themselves getting among the exhibits, to avoid their involvement in accidents. One of the few museums to show restoration in progress is the Mosquito Aircraft Museum, where the public can see, from behind a barrier, work on a Chipmunk, Tiger Moths, a Horsa Glider, possibly a Rapide and other de Havilland Aircraft. There is also a comprehensive display of de Havilland engines, in some cases sectioned, or being assembled.

Also at the Mosquito Museum local people mainly in the aerospace or airline industry work alongside others who have never touched an aircraft before joining the museum. Some even share their enthusiasm with members of their family, while others are happy just to provide working funds to make the museum a better place. The arrangement is by no means unique, rather it is an example of what goes on in many places. Nothing is too difficult and most enthusiasts dream of getting at least one of their aircraft in the air to make their effort all worthwhile.

If asked why they spend much of their spare time in relative discomfort restoring aircraft and engines, or repairing and painting buildings, few could give a clear answer. They are probably doing things they hate doing at home, or learning new skills. Office workers are doing manual labour, while a fitter might be helping to administer a supporters' group. The attraction is not only in the companionship of like-minded people, but also the challenge of achieving what initially appears impossible, and seeing the results of one's efforts being admired by the public. If at the same time money is being earned for a charity or other worthwhile cause then the achievement is that much greater.

Before finishing we must not forget the efforts of the private individuals working hard often in cramped conditions restoring some priceless aircraft to flying condition. In the British light aircraft movement, of course, de Havillands and Austers must come to mind first and both have their own fan clubs or owners' societies. The most recent to be formed is the de Havilland Moth Club which in addition to exchanging parts and knowledge for mutual benefit, has also, in August 1976 organised its first successful members' flying meeting.

Dynairship - freighter of the future?

PATRICK ABBOTT
Illustrations supplied by the author

AIRSHIPS, unlike balloons, possess two sources of lift; the static lift of the enclosed gas may be supplemented by the dynamic lift which is obtained when a dirigible is flown in a nose-up attitude. The whole envelope then acts as an aerofoil or wing and provides an amount of lift which varies according to the angle and the airspeed.

The extra lift can be substantial, even in airships of cylindrical form, which are not of the best shape to take full advantage of the dynamic lift factor. The German zeppelin L30, for example, which was the prototype for many subsequent German, British and American airships, possessed a gross static lift of about 59 tons, of which about 26 tons was disposable lift for fuel, ballast, payload and crew. However, flying at an angle of six degrees and at an airspeed of 45mph, the dynamic lift amounted to more than 2½ tons. Not only does this aspect of dirigible performance enable extra weight to be carried but, as it can be operated in reverse, to reduce lift, it enables airships to climb, dive, swoop and soar without the need to be constantly dropping ballast or releasing gas.

Occasional attempts have been made to design airships which make more use of dynamic lift by adopting a shape different from the orthodox circular cross-section used by nearly all normal dirigibles. Such vessels — half aeroplane, half aerostat — are sometimes nowadays called dynairships and they have attracted a certain amount of attention in recent years, although they are actually a type of craft which has aroused interest since long before either aeroplanes or airships were separately successful.

Probably the first-ever suggestion for an aircraft of the dynairship type was that of a Frenchman, Joseph Pline, in 1855. His proposed craft was to have been driven by no fewer than six propellers and was like a single huge wing containing many separate cells of gas. He named his project the Aeroplane — the first occasion that the word was used — and it was a machine at least a century ahead of its time.

Another rather similar idea was that of John Beugger, a Swiss. In 1888 he planned a dirigible balloon shaped like a biconvex lens and supported internally by a framework of rods. A car was suspended beneath the gasbag and carried two four-blade propellers powered by separate motors. The aircraft was to be steered either by varying the relative speeds of the propellers or by means of a rudder placed at the rear of the envelope. An adjustable weight controlled the longitudinal trim, so causing the balloon to rise or descend; or the same result was to be obtained by increasing or decreasing the speed. But the central and most noteworthy feature of the design was that the weight of the aircraft was deliberately planned to be greater than could be raised by the static lift of the gas alone, since the machine was intended to fly only when forward motion gave additional dynamic lift. As a take-off run would therefore be necessary — even if only a short one — the inventor suggested that his aircraft should be launched from a track of rails inclined slightly upwards.

Other projects based on the same combination of principles followed in due course. Two particularly attractive designs which were effectively both aeroplanes and airships were those of the Frenchman Adolphe Clement and the German Ernst Bucher, in 1907 and 1909. The former was one large wing, fashioned in the form of a perfectly circular lens, with its maximum thickness equal to one-sixth of the diameter and positioned one-third of the diameter from the leading edge. At the centre of the trailing edge was a single rectangular elevator, while similar control surfaces acted as ailerons at the wing tips. A vertical fin extended above and below the trailing edge, immediately in front of the elevator, and four sliding weights on separate endless cords allowed the aircraft to be trimmed longitudinally or laterally.

It was intended to construct the aircraft by having a framework of metal rings and rods covered with fabric, in a manner rather similar to that used by conventional rigid airships. And just as the rigid dirigibles used separate gasbags inside one hull, so the Clement machine was to have had four separate annular balloons, arranged concentrically and each divided up by internal partitions. The only feature to spoil the beautiful symmetry of this 'flying saucer' was the engine gondola which, of necessity, was suspended well below the hull and contained engines driving two propellers rotating in opposite directions to eliminate torque reaction. Sadly, Adolphe Clement never made his strange aircraft but turned his attention instead to non-rigid dirigibles of conventional form. In that he

Specification of the Adolphe Clement project of 1907.

Fig. 1.

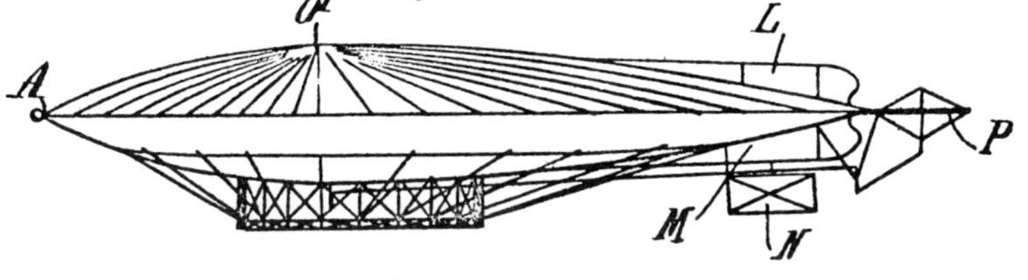

Fig. 2.

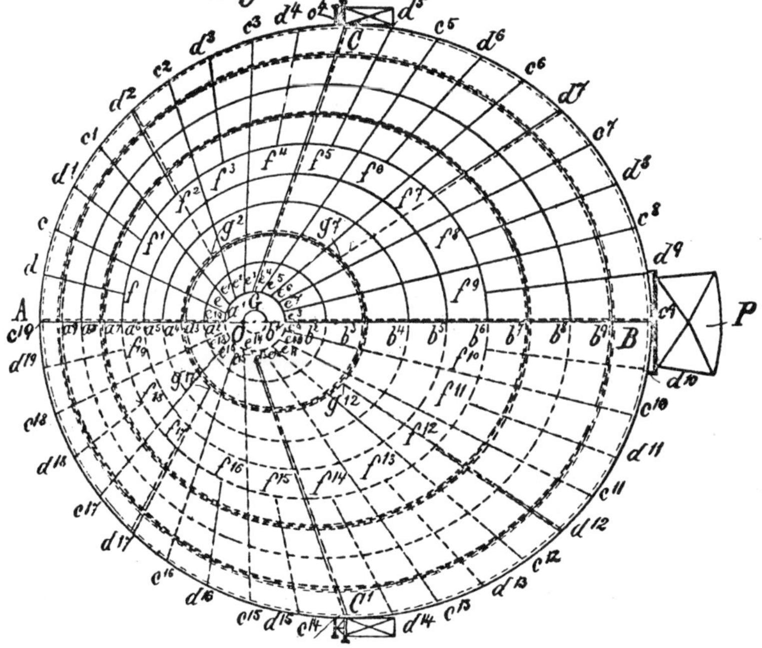

Fig. 3.

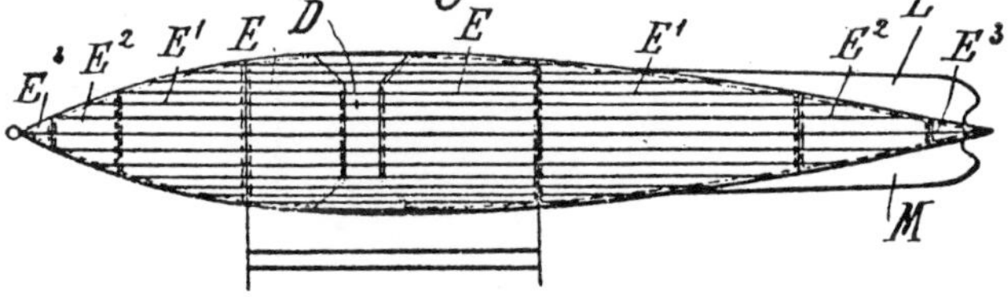

Fig. 4.

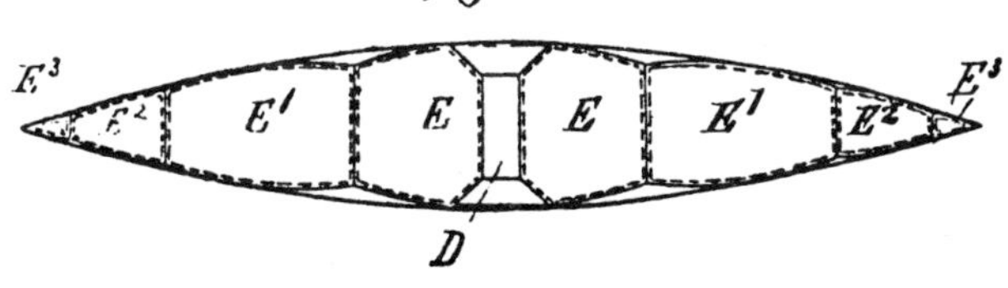

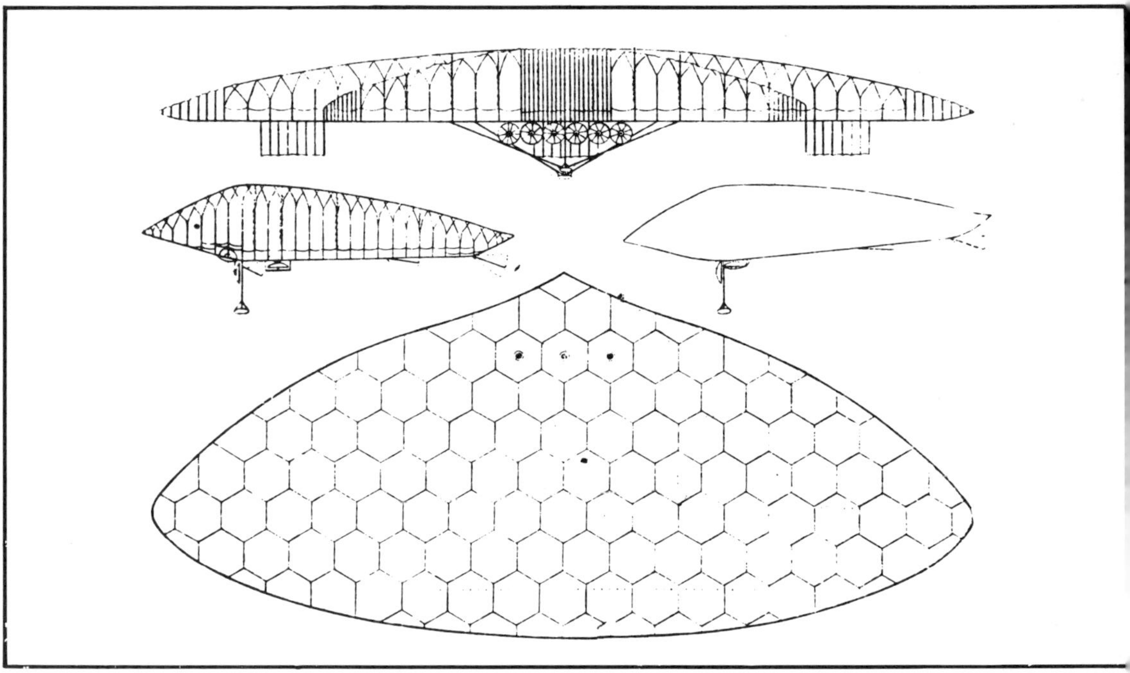

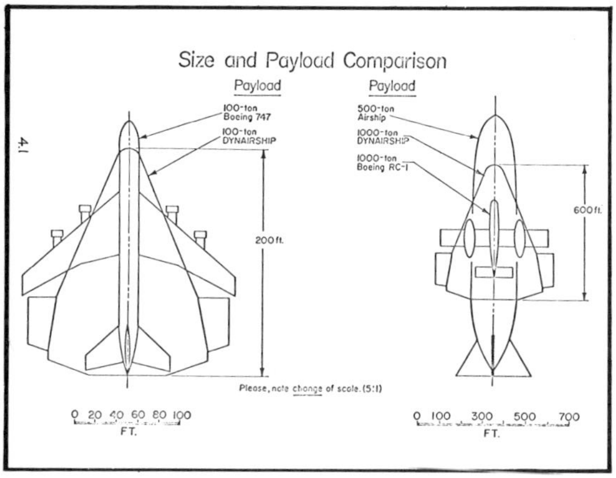

Left: Outline of Joseph Pline's 1855 proposal.

Below left: The small-scale prototype built by Aereon Corporation, Aereon 26.

Above: Size and payload comparisons of various aircraft, airship and dynairship designs, prepared by the Aereon Corporation.

was more successful and one of his craft, with the inventor aboard, made the first airship crossing of the English Channel in October 1910.

The Bucher machine — designed by an optician — was also of rigid construction, but of elliptical form with flattened sides and containing four internal gasbags arranged one to each quadrant. One elevator was attached to the nose of the aircraft and two others flanked a rectangular rudder at the rear. The gondola was fastened underneath the centre of the vessel and it contained an engine driving three propellers, one immediately in front and two others at the extreme tips of the huge lenticular wings. The wing-tip propellers pivoted so that they could provide either lift or propulsion, as well as an aid to manoeuvring.

Both of those Edwardian aircraft were advanced designs that embodied ingenious features. But as with their predecessors, neither moved any nearer to reality than the Patent Office, and like several other attempts to combine the virtues of the aeroplane with the advantages of the aerostat, they proved sadly abortive. Not for more than a generation was such a vessel actually built.

It was nearly two decades after the end of WW2 when a group of Americans — mostly naval airship veterans — formed a company to develop a new form of aircraft which would be able to carry heavy freight over long distances with economy and safety. Led first by Monroe Drew and later by William Miller (both, oddly enough, theologians) they called their project the Aereon, taking both the name and their inspiration from an outwardly similar flying machine that their compatriot, Solomon Andrews, had invented almost exactly a century earlier. The Aereon Corporation planned eventually to build enormous aircraft carrying many tons of cargo, but as such vessels were quite beyond their limited means, a much smaller version was produced as a preliminary exercise.

It became known as the Aereon 3 (the number being derived from the triple configuation) and took the form of an airship with three streamlined hulls, each 80 feet long and with a maximum diameter of 18 feet joined together longitudinally like an aerial trimaran. Two pivoting control surfaces were fitted at the rear and these 'elevons' acted in unison as elevators or in opposition as ailerons. Fins and rudders were provided beneath the two outer hulls and a four-cylinder two-stroke McCullough engine of 92hp drove a pusher propeller at the rear of the central hull. At the forward end was a cockpit protected by a Plexiglas canopy and containing seats for two pilots. In order to obtain good ground stability, a tricycle undercarriage of very wide track and long wheelbase was used. The whole aircraft, weighing about 3300lb, was covered with white-painted fabric and held 50,000 cubic feet of helium contained in plastic bags and giving a static lift of just over 3000lb.

The building of the Aereon 3 took a long time, and not until 15 April 1966 was it ready for a maiden flight that proved sadly abortive. On an airfield in Mercer County the craft was brought from its hangar and cautiously taxied forward without regard for a stiff crosswind that threatened its buoyant instability. Suddenly aware that he would be unable to slow down and stop before reaching the end of the runway, the pilot was obliged to swing the aircraft sharply round, tilting it sideways and allowing the wind to catch at the broad expanse of the undersurface. As the Aereon 3 keeled over, the pilot leapt out through the entrance hatch, despite being 18 feet above the ground. Then the unfortunate aircraft crashed on its back and the second pilot also jumped down, smashing his way to safety straight through the Plexiglas canopy. Deprived of their stabilising weight, the craft was immediately overturned once more by the wind, and its delicately welded framework crumpled beyond hope of repair; thus years of patient work were wasted in a few disastrous moments.

In spite of that bitter disappointment, the men of the Aereon Corporation had no intention of abandoning

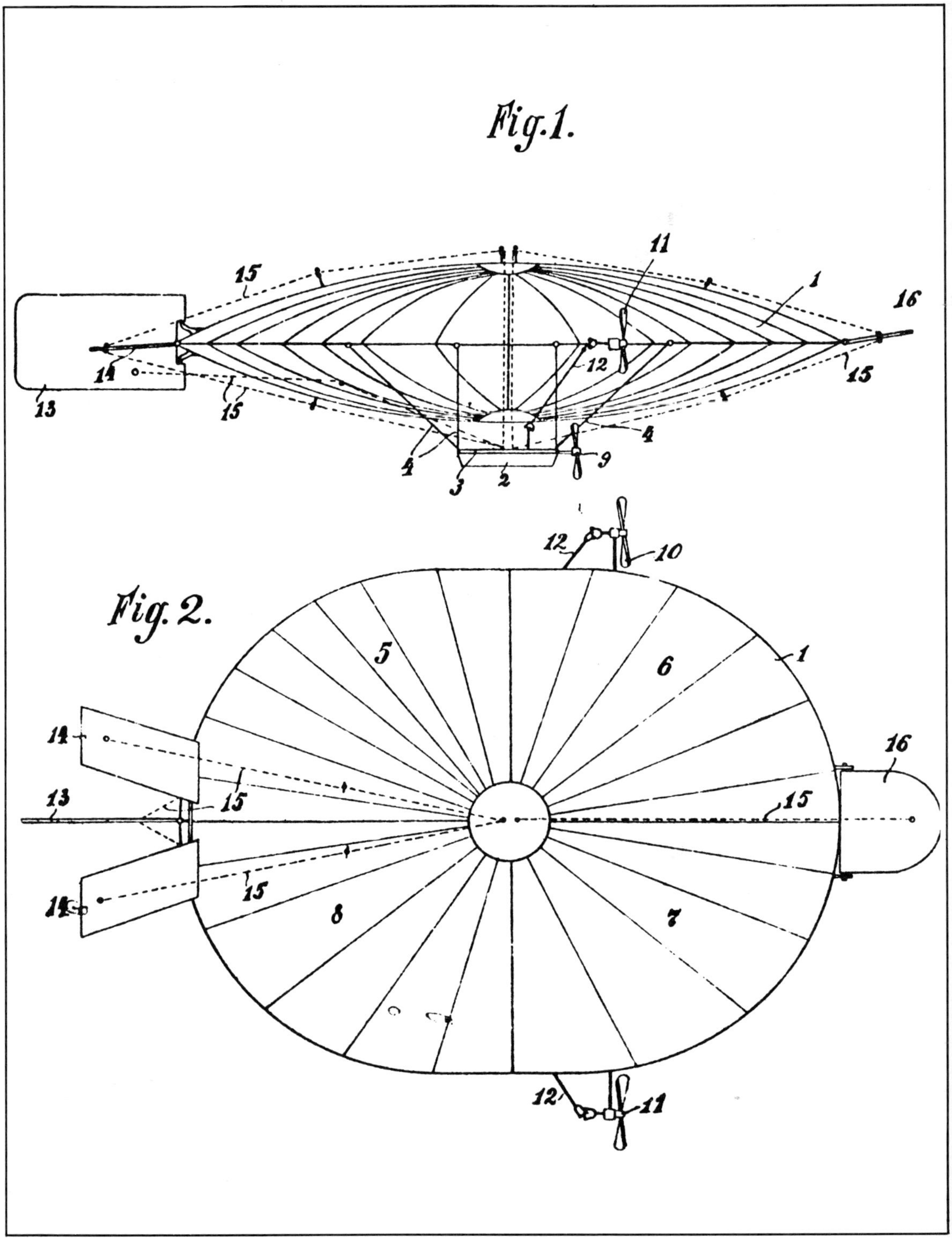
Fig.1.
1
2
3
4
9
11
12
13
14
15
16
Fig. 2.
1
5
6
7
8
10
11
12
13
14
15
16

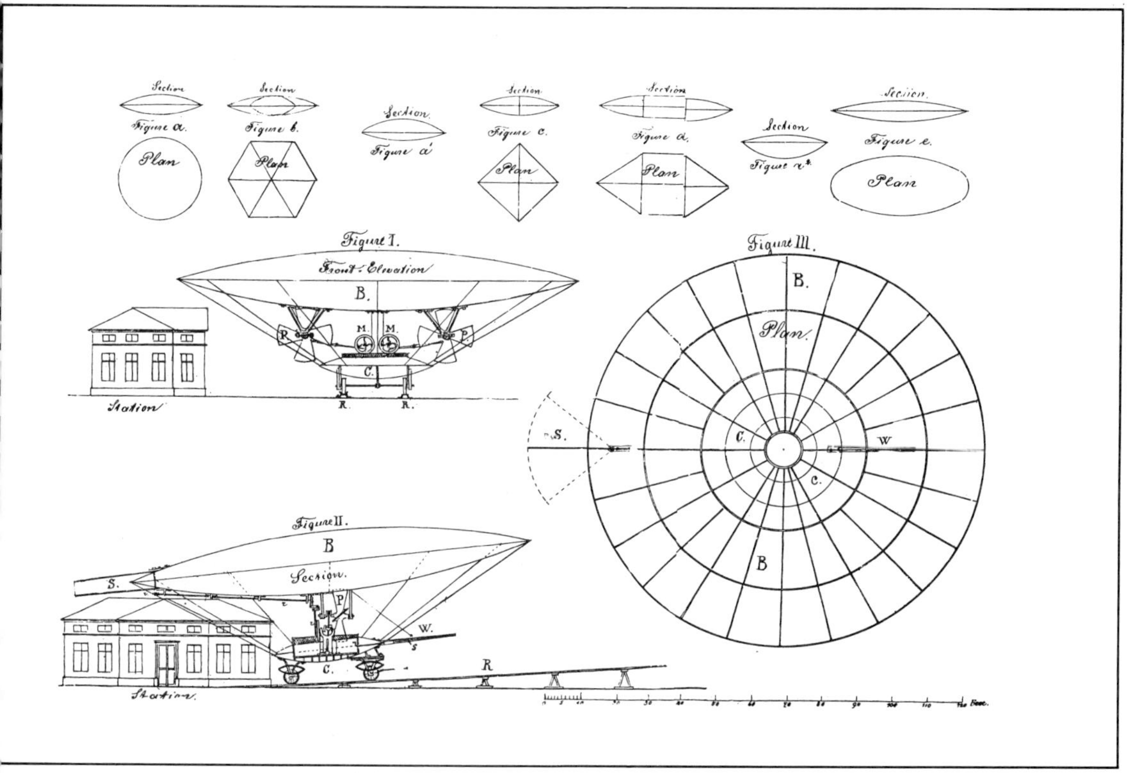

Left: Ernst Bucher's specification of 1910.

Above: John Beuggar's proposals of 1888.

heir project. The requirements which they sought to atisfy were put to a computer, in order to obtain the hape which should most efficiently combine the ttributes of the aeroplane and the airship. Data of 17 lifferent criteria were fed into the computer and its erdict brought an abrupt end to the triple-hulled onfiguration. Instead the very different form uggested was a triangular shape of deep cross-section ot very dissimilar to that proposed by Joseph Pline nore than a hundred years before.

The new shape, known colloquially as the deltoid umpkin seed, gave high dynamic and static lift, yet airly low drag; for this new style of aircraft the eneric term dynairship was coined. Experiments were arried out with a radio-controlled model, the Aereon 7, and also with small rubber-powered machines. Eventually, after many months of research and desperate fund raising, a man-carrying version, the Aereon 26, was duly designed and built. The designation number derived from the original estimate of its length, but length was later increased slightly and the completed craft measured 27 feet long and had a span of 24 feet and a weight of 1140lb. By coincidence the aircraft registration figures incorporated the planned and actual lengths into one number — N2627. Not a bolt nor a rivet was used in the construction, which was a totally welded structure of aluminium tubing, and while the internal capacity was 20 times that of a light aeroplane of comparable length, the weight was only half as much.

The engine, driving a rear-mounted pusher propeller, had been salvaged from the Aereon 3, with several other items of equipment from the earlier vessel. The fabric covering was painted bright orange with black markings and the machine was provided with seating for one pilot only. The aircraft was intended only as a small-scale prototype for a much larger craft, where the volume of gas, increasing as the cube of the linear dimension, would provide a degree of static lift equivalent to the weight of the structure. In a miniature prototype such as the Aereon 26 the

Two illustrations prepared by the Aereon Corporation showing general and internal views of its projected full-size dynairship of 1000 tons payload capacity.

amount of lift would inevitably be of only marginal effect and for that reason, therefore, it was decided to fly the machine solely as a wingless heavier-than-air craft, or 'aerobody', in order to obtain data on handling and performance characteristics.

On 6 September 1970, on a New Jersey airfield, the Aereon 26 made several short hops, piloted with careful skill by John Olcott. But although the aerobody lifted off easily and flew with encouraging stability, it was unable to rise more than a few feet above the ground. Further trials during the following days showed that the craft was too underpowered to escape the ground effect and could rise no more than a dozen feet above the runway.

In an effort to break through the barrier the aerobody was lightened drastically; the radio, fire extinguisher, parachute and half of the fuel supply were sacrificed in order to reduce weight, as well as several minor items of equipment. A fortnight later, on 28 September, Olcott tried again, this time with rather more success as the Aereon 26 reached a speed of about 65mph and an altitude of 50 feet or more. Nevertheless, the performance was still disappointingly below expectations and it was clear that more effective use of the existing power output was essential if any significant results were to be achieved.

A delay of seven months then ensued while a more efficient propeller was designed and made; it was a four-blade version hand-carved from yellow birch and only four feet in diameter. Finally, on 1 March 1971, all was ready and the Aereon 26, again piloted by John Olcott, made several short flights at very low altitude. All went well and so preparations were made for a full trial on the following Saturday, 6 March. This time there was no disappointment and John Olcott successfully lifted off the Aereon 26 at a speed of just under 60mph and slowly climbed to an altitude of 500 feet before levelling off and reaching a top speed of nearly 75mph. Then he flew three or four times in a wide circuit of the airfield and its environs before bringing the aerobody in to a smooth landing. During the following days, more flights were made, flights which were slow and unspectacular but which confirmed in practice the theoretical value of the dynairship concept. Once having proved its viability, the Aereon 26 had fulfilled its only purpose and so it was stored away, never to fly again.

But even before the practical justification of their ideas, the men of the Aereon Corporation had prepared plans for full-size dynairships — enormous delta-wing aircraft with an airframe that was at one aerofoil, gasbag, cargo hold, crew compartment and engine room. It was envisaged that such an aircraft would measure up to perhaps 1000 feet in length and that the enclosed helium would balance the weight of the structure, so that the dynamic lift would enable loads of the order of 1000 tons to be carried.

The fully developed dynairship was planned to have a symmetrical profile, the angle of attack necessary to produce dynamic lift being obtained by the action of the elevators. The delta-shaped hull — with a length greater than its span — was constructed of aluminium panels and supported by a stiffening framework. At

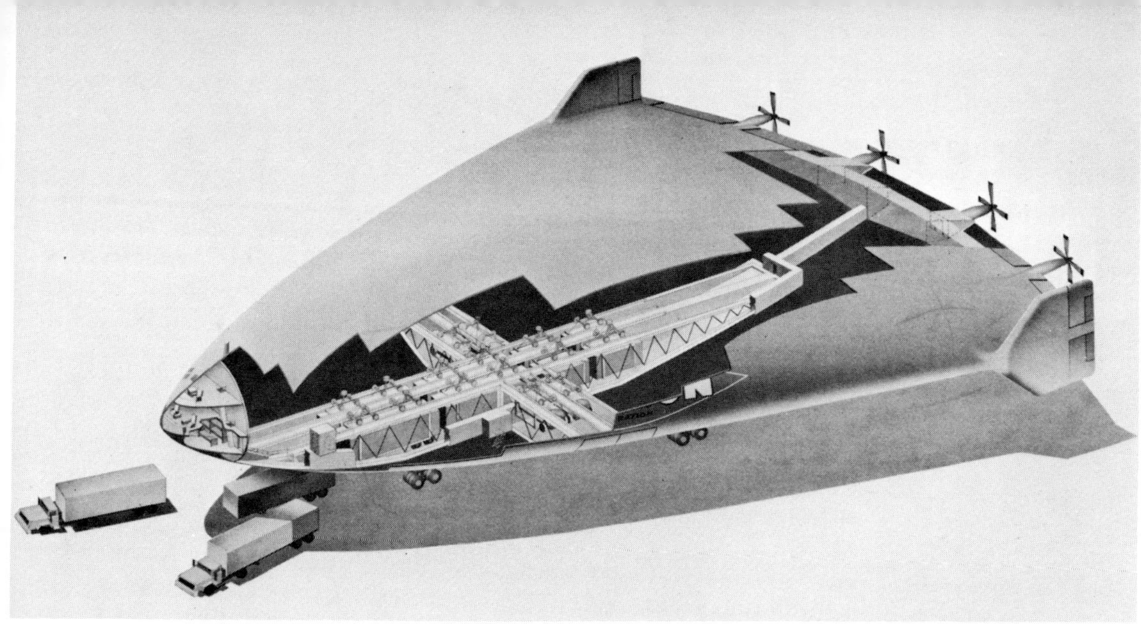

the rear of the hull were four turboprop engines, positioned so that the best airflow characteristics were obtained. The interior of the dynairship formed a single huge gas container, with flight decks, access corridors and quarters for the crew partitioned off at the nose and elsewhere.

A large cargo and fuel compartment was suspended internally by steel cables which distributed the load over a large area of the upper shell of the body, the fuel supply being contained in two sections on each side of the cargo hold. The cargo itself was to be containerised, probably in the form of eight large trailer bodies, and supported by hoists riding on rails running lengthwise in the aircraft. Two cargo supporting tracks were provided, so that one track might be unloaded and then reloaded before the process was repeated with the other. By always keeping one track weighted, the vessel was prevented from becoming dangerously buoyant.

In addition to a nose-wheel assembly and small wheels on the underside of each fin, eight multiple-wheel units, all retractable, were provided and placed successively farther apart towards the rear, for lateral stability. The wheels swivelled freely about the vertical axis, so permitting cross-wind landings, since there was no necessity for the dynairship to be aligned exactly with the runway. The landing gear was also selectively adjustable for height, a feature which enabled the vessel to assume a nose-up attitude for take-off or a nose-down attitude while on the ground.

In order that the aircraft might be taxied backwards, to avoid sharp turns or to remain facing nose-down into a strong wind, a control station was provided at the extreme rear. A further use was also found for the nose-wheel assembly; it provided a tie-down point for ground mooring, allowing the vessel to weathervane on its swivelling undercarriage units in a manner similar to the way traditional airships once swung their bows into the wind when tied to high mooring masts.

The Aereon Corporation maintained that the gigantic aircraft belied its apparent clumsiness by virtue of compromising nicely between the very different disadvantages suffered by conventional cargo-carrying aeroplanes and airships. The conventional aircraft can taxi and requires a minimum number of men in the ground crew, but it inevitably has fast and potentially dangerous landing and take-off speeds. Above all, it needs long smooth uninterrupted runways. The airship, although able to do without large landing fields, is unable to taxi and requires complex mooring, landing and take-off operations as well as very large handling parties.

By comparison, the Aereon dynairship would be able to use small landing fields with ease, move on the ground without external assistance, and have a wide speed range, giving both safety of handling and efficiency of operation. These and many other features of the Aeron design would have produced a freight-carrying vessel with unique and remarkable qualities.

Unfortunately, the cost of constructing even one full-size prototype was assessed at many millions of dollars and was far beyond the slender resources of the impecunious Aereon Corporation. All attempts to persuade the American Congress or industry to advance such a sum proved unavailing and the project is now in abeyance. To all appearances, the Aereon machines are not only better publicised, better planned but equally unrealised repetitions of the designs of Pline, Beugger, Clement, Bucher and several other visionaries. Yet it is difficult to believe that this is really the end of the story.

Collectors' Corner

PHILIP JARRETT

All pictures in this feature supplied by the compiler

Vickers Wellesley 1 L2673 of 223 Sqn RAF in flight over Mount Kenya, East Africa, circa 1938/40. Powered by a 950hp Bristol Pegasus XX air-cooled radial engine, the Wellesley was a two/three-seat high-performance bomber and general-purpose monoplane, employing the geodetic construction originally evolved by Barnes Wallis for airships. The first RAF unit to re-equip with the type was No 76 (Bomber) Sqn in 1937. No 223 Sqn received its first Wellesleys in June 1938, and they took part in the East African Campaign from bases at Summit and Wadi Gazonza, Sudan, the squadron finally parting with them in April 1941. Visible in this picture are the streamlined underwing containers for 2000lb of bombs, and the manner in which the gunner's transparency hinged upwards at the front.

Left: One of America's greatest aerial stuntmen, 28-year-old Harry 'Tex' McLaughlin, hangs by his teeth from a trapeze suspended from the undercarriage of a Canuck, the Canadian-built version of the Curtiss JN4 'Jenny' trainer, in 1920. This particular trick was one of McLaughlin's specialities — and he used to spin around with arms and legs outstretched to add to the entertainment! He also changed aircraft in mid-air.

Below left: 'Tex' McLaughlin dangles beneath a Canuck while blindfolded, one of the positions from which he accomplished a change of aircraft, still wearing the blindfold! His daring finally led to his downfall, for he was fatally injured on 20 September 1921 while changing planes before 50,000 spectators at the New York State Fair in Syracuse.

Below: Despite its looks, the d'Ascanio helicopter of 1930 was a successful machine in its time. In October 1930 its Italian inventor, C d'Ascanio, flew it to a world altitude record of 59ft, a distance record of 1180yd and an endurance record of 8min 45sec for helicopters. Eventually acquired by the Italian Air Ministry, it had a 95hp Fiat A50 engine which drove a pair of two-bladed co-axial contra-rotating rotors and three small variable-pitch propellers — one for lateral control, one on the tail for longitudinal control, and the third for yaw control. At the tip of each rotor blade was a small 'tailplane' which acted as stabiliser and an elevator operable from the cockpit to change blade pitch.

Top: Designed to meet the requirements of Air Ministy Specification M1/30 for a torpedo-bomber ship-plane to replace the Fleet Air Arm's Blackburn Ripons, the unnamed Vickers M1/30 was photographed complete with dummy torpedo in 1933 at Brooklands, where it was built. Accommodating a pilot and observer, the M1/30 was powered by an 825hp Rolls-Royce Buzzard IIIMS engine, and its 50ft-span wings incorporated constructional techniques developed for the R100 airship by Barnes Wallis and later used throughout the Wellesley. The M1/30 first flew at Brooklands on 11 January 1933 and made 23 flights before crashing after suffering a structural failure in flight on 23 November the same year. Fortunately, both pilot and passenger parachuted to safety.

Above: The prototype Miles M3 Falcon Major, G-ACTM, taxies out on 18 October 1934. Powered by a 120hp de Havilland Gipsy Major engine, the Falcon was built for Mr H L Brook of Harrogate to fly in the MacRobertson Race from England to Australia, and made its first flight on 12 October 1934 in the hands of F G Miles. Its engine had previously been installed in Mr Brook's Puss Moth G-ABXY, which James Mollison had flown across the Atlantic. As entry No 31 in the race, which began at Mildenhall on 20 October 1934, the Falcon met with ill fortune, taking 27 days to reach Darwin. For the return flight to Lympne, however, Brook achieved a record time of seven days, 19hr 15min, including a 1700-mile non-stop flight between Jodhpur and Basra. Two years later G-ACTM ended its life in a crash in November 1936.

Above: Handling crewmen steady a Fairey Swordfish Mk 1 of the first production batch as it is lowered by crane on to a catapult at one of the Fleet Air Arm land-based training schools in October 1941. The aeroplane's 750hp Bristol Pegasus III M3 radial engine is already running, as it had to be turned by a hand-inertia starter (hard work for a couple of 'erks'!), and this could only be accomplished while the aircraft was on the ground. Also visible is the extended headrest, which prevented the pilot's head from being jerked back as the aircraft was fired from the catapult. After their training pilots were sent to fly Swordfish from catapults mounted on ships, to protect convoys from the dreaded German U-boats.

Right: A fine take-off study of Douglas DC3B-G102 Skysleeper NC17314 of Transcontinental and Western Air (later Trans World Airlines). This aircraft, constructor's No 1924, joined TWA in May 1937 with the fleet number 352. During World War 2 it served with the United States Air Force as 42-57511, returning to TWA with its original registration on 17 October 1944. As N17314 it then passed to Transocean Airlines and on to the Union Steel & Wrecking Co on 16 January 1953. Its next owner was General Airways, and during its time with that operator it was used in the film *Island in the Sky*, bearing 'USAF' serial 1048. N17314 was finally destroyed by fire at Kerrville, Texas, on 2 February 1959.

Above: Another classic airliner, this time the Ford 4/AT-B Tri-Motor NC7121 (constructor's No 4/AT-35), powered by a trio of 675hp Wright J5 radial engines. This amazing picture was taken over Miami, Florida, in February 1930, while the aircraft was serving with Tri-Motored Air Tours Inc of Port Clinton, Ohio, who operated it until 1936. In case readers wonder if it was normal for mechanics to dangle from a cable beneath the tailplane, a caption on the back of the photograph states that Mr James Terry was proving the worth of his new invention, which enabled a rudder control cable to be repaired in four minutes while the aircraft was in flight. In the author's opinion, if you believe that, you'll believe anything; particularly as the control cables run along the top of the fuselage and above the tailplane — completely beyond Mr Terry's reach! The probable truth is that he was following the footsteps of 'Tex' McLaughlin. In 1938 NC7121 joined the Columbia Picture Corp of California at Hollywood, and appeared in the film *Only Angels Have Wings.* From 1939-40 it was with United Air Services Ltd at Burbank, California.

Above right: Boeing 377 Stratocruiser N1028V *Clipper Flying Cloud* of Pan American World Airways touches down at London (Heathrow) Airport at 13.25 on Monday, 4 April 1949 after its maiden transatlantic crossing from New York. The first of its type to visit the UK, it was the fourth of 20 Stratocruisers to be delivered to Pan Am, which company it joined on 14 March 1949. N1028V was traded back to Boeing in 1961 and then sold to a company called Mansdorf, later passing to the Venezuelan company Rutas Aereas Nacionales SA (RANSA) as YV-C-ERG, who fitted it with a cargo door. It was finally broken up at Miami in June 1969.

Right: Hawker Hart Trainer K6515, built by Armstrong Whitworth, crashed in a field at Mollington near Chester, on 6 June 1939. It was serving at Sealand with No 5 Flying Training School RAF at the time, and both pilot and pupil escaped serious injury. Powered by a 525hp Rolls-Royce Kestrel IB engine, the Hart Trainer was evolved to prepare pilots for operational flying on the Hart light day-bomber, already in service with the RAF. The first Hart Trainer made its maiden flight on 20 April 1932 and 303 were built by Armstrong Whitworth.

PAN AMERICAN WORLD AIRWAYS

Below: Flying over Southampton Water on 30 July 1939, Flight Refuelling Ltd's appropriately registered Handley Page Harrow tanker, G-AFRL, and Short S30 flying-boat G-AFCU *Cabot* of Imperial Airways demonstrate the technique of in-flight refuelling. Previously K7027, Harrow G-AFRL was fitted with fuselage tanks having a capacity of 1000gal, and was one of the aircraft used to refuel the Empire flying-boats during weekly transatlantic airmail services from Southampton to New York, refuelling taking place over Foynes and Botwood. These flights started on 8 August 1939 and eight round trips were made before war ended the service. G-AFRL was destroyed at Ford during an air raid on 18 August 1940.

Right: Australian-registered Simmonds Spartan VH-UIT, powered by a 95hp ADC Cirrus III engine, was one of 48 examples produced; it was one of five sold in Australia in 1929 by Spartan agent Robt Bryce & Co Pty Ltd. The first Spartan was flown in mid-1928, and late in the year production started at Weston, Southampton. For economy all four wing panels and ailerons were identical and had symmetrical aerofoil sections, enabling a replacement wing panel to fit in any of the four positions. In addition the rudder was interchangeable with either elevator, each half of the undercarriage would fit on either side, and all the main bracing wires were of the same length. But potential buyers were wary of the symmetrical wing section because of its alleged spinning tendencies. VH-UIT, c/n 3, was first registered in February 1929 and was owned variously before being struck off the Australian register on 12 October 1939.

Below right: Another inter-war Aussie, this time the five-seat Stinson SR-8B Reliant VH-UXL. Built in 1930 by the Stinson Aircraft Corporation at Wayne, Michigan, USA, and powered by a 245hp Lycoming R680-B6 radial engine, the Reliant was a popular cabin monoplane of the late 1930s. Here the machine is seen when owned by Vacuum Oil Co Pty Ltd, Melbourne, during 1937-39. It was impressed into RAAF service in 1940. Reregistered in 1948, it still survives as part of the Joe Drage collection at Wodonga, Victoria.

VH-UIT

VH-UXL

Scottish Aviation Twin Pioneer of J F Airlines silhouetted by a setting sun at Portsmouth in 1972./*Mike Jerram*